Solid
BLACK and WHITE
ANSWERS

To Life's Questions

Mike Moskau

2d-Ra-Ha-Je-Says-It-All

Mike Moskau

Harvard House
Golden, Colorado

Printed in the United States of America

Unless otherwise noted, Scriptures quoted from The Holy Bible, New Century Version, copyright ©1987, 1988, 1991 by Word Publishing, Dallas, Texas 75039. Used by permission.

Scripture quotations noted NKJV are from the New King James Version of the Bible. Copyright ©1979, 1980, 1982, Thomas Nelson, Inc., Publishers. Used by permission.

Scripture quotations noted TLB are from *The Living Bible* (Wheaton, Illinois: Tyndale House Publishers, 1971). Used by permission.

ISBN: 0-9640404-8-4

Edited and cover design by Linda Moskau

Contents

*Dedicated to Mom (in memory)
and Dad who, through their lives,
planted the seeds of Christianity
in their children.*

Acknowledgment

I know now why God saved the best for me. He had plans for this book and knew I needed the best of help. My remarkable wife has labored unselfishly on this project many, many hours. Her skills in English, editing and desk top publishing have been the best.
Thank you very much, Linda.

Introduction

Chances are the devil knows more of what's in the Bible than you do. There is a fierce spiritual battle going on over your eternal soul and evil forces are doing everything in their power to make you defenseless. Their priority is to keep you from knowing the inspired absolute truth that is found in God's Word, the Bible.

If the Bible can be proven to be inspired truth, then the words in the Book become of utmost importance. The words are significant because they can answer critical questions about everyday life and can instruct people how to get to heaven.

The books in the Bible were written down by men, but they were inspired by God so the words said precisely what God wanted them to say. Proving that these words are inspired can be done through archaeological evidence, prophecy, manuscript evidence and the science of statistical probability. Knowing that the words of the Bible contain what people are looking for, the truth, you would think everyone would be searching the Scriptures for answers. However, a *USA Today* Gallup poll revealed only 11% of people read their Bible. That means most people, from first hand knowledge, don't know what's in this important book. Depending on others to tell you the truth of what's in the Holy Bible is not wise because it's **your** eternal life that's at stake. The book of Matthew, Chapter 7, states only a **few** people make it to heaven. **That means the things most people are depending on to get them to heaven are incorrect!**

The familiar saying of, "If you want something done right you have to do it yourself," certainly holds true here. If you want to know the answers to life's questions and the correct steps it takes to enter heaven, then you must get this truth from the Bible yourself.

The focus of this book is for you to get answers directly from God. I pose the questions, with occasional comments, but I use an easy to understand translation of God's Word to answer the questions.

This statement believed by many to be true is not. "You can get to heaven by being good or going to church." Why that statement is false and answers to over 800 questions are answered in the following pages direct from the source of truth—God's Word, the Holy Bible.

"Enter through the narrow gate. The gate is wide and the road is wide that leads to hell, and many people enter through that gate. But the gate is small and the road is narrow that leads to true life. Only a few people find that road."

Words of Jesus, Matthew 7:13-14

Chapter One

**"A thorough knowledge of the Bible is worth more
than a college education."**
- Theodore Roosevelt -

■ **What is the purpose of life?**

"Bring to me all the people who are mine, <u>whom I [God] made for my
glory</u> [emphasis added], whom I call and made." Isaiah 43:7

*Life is difficult but it does not have to be a mystery. Now that you have
discovered what the purpose for being is, the next step would be to dig
into the "owner's manual" for life, the Holy Bible, and uncover what
God's purposes are for your existence.*

■ **Is the Bible, God's Word, too difficult to understand?**

"The teaching that I [Jesus] ask you to accept is easy; the load I give you
to carry is light." Matthew 11:30

■ **What is the most important message of the entire Bible?**

I passed on to you what I received, of which this was most important:
that Christ died for our sins, as the Scriptures say; that he was buried
and was raised to life on the third day . . . . I Corinthians 15:3, 4

■ **Do you feel like such a terrible sinner that you are not worthy of
being forgiven or loved by God? WRONG! You are exactly who
Jesus is looking for.**

"Why do you eat and drink with tax collectors and sinners?" Jesus answered them, "It is not the healthy people who need a doctor, but the sick. I have not come to invite good people but sinners to change their hearts and lives." Luke 5:30, 32

■ **There have been many books written, but how many have been inspired by God?**

All Scripture is given by inspiration of God . . . . II Timothy 3:16 NKJV

Only the sixty-six books that make up the Holy Bible have been inspired by God. The word "inspired" can also be translated "God-breathed." The Bible was written by men but since it was inspired, everything was put down just as if God had penned it himself!

■ **People will argue that the Bible was just written by ordinary men. About 40 ordinary men, as a matter-of-fact, but let them try arguing this question. The Bible had many writers, but didn't it have only one Author?**

<u>All</u> Scripture is given by God [emphasis added] and is useful for teaching, for showing people what is wrong in their lives, for correcting faults, and for teaching how to live right. II Timothy 3:16

■ **Is there proof that the Bible is true and God is the author?**

Who is a God like me? That God should come and prove it. Let him tell and explain all that has happened since I set up my ancient people. <u>He should also tell what will happen in the future</u> [emphasis added]. Isaiah 44:7

No one but God can predict 100% accurately what will happen in the future. The Bible chronicles history in advance. Of the hundreds of predicted events that have come to pass, not one has been in error. There is nothing comparable in all other religious writings because they don't even attempt predicting future events. Predicting future history without error confirms the Bible is God's Word. To help you see the difficulty in forecasting history in advance let's try a little predicting ourselves. Pick the football team, including any new future teams, that will win the Super Bowl in the year 4458. That is an example of what God did 2600 years ago when He said, in advance, Israel would disappear as a nation but then would miraculously become a country again in the last days. On May 14, 1948, Israel became a modern nation!

For the time is coming when I will restore the fortunes of my people, Israel and Judah, and I will bring them home to this land that I gave to their fathers; they shall possess it and live here again [written about 600 B.C.]. Jeremiah 30:3 TLB

■ **What wise words of Solomon could change your whole life, especially if you are married?**

A gentle answer will calm a person's anger, but an unkind answer will cause more anger. Proverbs 15:1

■ **Are you neutral about God? Is God neutral about you?**

"Whoever is not with me [God] is against me. Whoever does not work with me is working against me." Matthew 12:30

■ **People do some pretty horrendous things. Can they be forgiven for each and every sin?**

"So I tell you, people can be forgiven for every sin and everything they say against God." Matthew 12:31

The "unforgivable sin" is addressed later.

■ **Do some of our common sayings we use today, such as "the blind leading the blind" come from the Bible?**

Stay away from the Pharisees; they are blind leaders. And if a blind person leads a blind person, both will fall into a ditch. Matthew 15:14

Another common saying we use is, "The handwriting is on the wall."

Suddenly the fingers of a person's hand appeared and began writing on the plaster of the wall . . . . The king watched the hand as it wrote. King

Belshazzar was very frightened. His face turned white, his knees knocked together, and he could not stand up because his legs were too weak. Daniel 5:5-6

■ **Feeling a little low about yourself? If you are a true Christian look what's in store for you.**

"I tell you, John [the Baptist] is greater than any other person ever born, but even the least important person in the kingdom of God is greater than John." Luke 7:28

■ **Does nudity and the devil have anything in common?**

. . . a man from the town who had demons inside him came to Jesus. For a long time he had worn no clothes . . . . Luke 8:27

■ **Is pizza mentioned in the Bible? It should be; I think it's heavenly. How about deviled ham; is it mentioned?**

A large herd of pigs was feeding on a hill and the demons begged Jesus to allow them to go into the pigs. Jesus allowed them to do this. Luke 8:32

Wouldn't a story of how deviled ham got its name be entertaining for Paul Harvey's "The Rest of the Story" program? Hope you enjoy "Biblical" humor.

A happy heart is like good medicine, but a broken spirit drains your strength. Proverbs 17:22

■ **What is the only thing besides deviled ham the devil likes for lunch?**

Control yourselves and be careful! The devil, your enemy, goes around like a roaring lion looking for someone to eat. I Peter 5:8

That someone could be YOU! Filling yourself up with knowledge from the Bible gives the devil indigestion.

■ **Where is your life heading? What are you aiming for?**

. . . aim at what is in heaven, where Christ is sitting at the right hand of God. Colossians 3:1

■ **Do you need encouragement in fighting your battles?**

"Be strong and brave. Don't be afraid or worried because of the king of Assyria or his large army [substitute here your battles and problems]. There is a greater power with us than with him. He only has men, but we have the LORD our God to help us and to fight our battles." II Chronicles 32:7, 8

■ **With all the technological advances, why can't science extend the average life span beyond seventy to eighty years?**

Our lifetime is seventy years or, if we are strong, eighty years. Psalm 90:10

It's because the Creator has put a boundary on the number of our years.

■ **Do we marry in heaven? If we are married on earth will we have the same mate in heaven?**

"Since all seven men had married her, when people rise from the dead, whose wife will she be?" Jesus answered, "You don't understand, because you don't know what the Scriptures say . . . . When people rise from the dead, they will not marry, nor will they be given to someone to marry." Matthew 22:28-30

■ **Just how important is the truth? Is truth a major factor of whether you go to heaven or not?**

You are saved by the Spirit that makes you holy and by your faith in the truth. II Thessalonians 2:13

The truth is God's Word. Read it often.

■ **What is one important reason the Bible was written?**

Write these things for the future so that people who are not yet born will praise the LORD. Psalm 102:18

That means it was written down for you!

■ **What has been taught from the beginning that permeates the entire Bible?**

This is the teaching you have heard from the beginning: We must love each other. I John 3:11

■ **Stop! Look! and Listen! What is the key to life?**

My child, pay attention to my [God's] words; listen closely to what I say. Don't ever forget my words; keep them always in mind. They are the key to life for those who find them; they bring health to the whole body. Proverbs 4:20-22

Part of the idea behind this book is to give you a taste of all the great things in the Bible. If some of these wise sayings of Solomon from Proverbs sound good, there are hundreds more in your Bible.

■ **Do you find it hard to believe God has always existed? Don't feel bad, that is a tough one. This is how I deal with that ponderable question. As a Christian it is easy to believe I am going to live forever. So I just turn it around and say if I believe I can live forever in the future, then I believe God could have lived forever in the past.**

. . . and God, who has been alive forever, sat on his throne. Daniel 7:9

■ **Have people in cults or false religions been tricked by the devil?**

But I am afraid that your minds will be led away from your true and pure following of Christ just as Eve was tricked by the snake [the devil] with his evil ways. II Corinthians 11:3

■ **Is there anywhere in the Bible where it says that the Son of God [Jesus] is God?**

But God the only Son . . . . John 1:18

■ **How did Jesus prove He was God the Savior?**

The Jews gathered around him and said, "How long will you make us wonder about you? If you are the Christ, tell us plainly." Jesus answered, "I told you already but you did not believe. The miracles I do in my Father's name show who I am." John 10:24-25

■ **Why do unfortunate circumstances happen to Christians? The answer to this takes faith to trust God that even though we don't understand why certain things happen, we must understand that ultimately it is for our own good.**

And we know that all that happens to us is working for our good if we love God and are fitting into his plans. Romans 8:28 TLB

If someone went through a financial crisis and because of it they turned their life over to God, was that ultimately a good or bad thing that happened? Or if someone (include me here) went through a severe depression that brought them back to church and put them on fire to witness to lost souls, was that something good or bad that happened?

■ **Why were the Ten Commandments and the law given?**

So what was the law for? It was given to show that the wrong things people do are against God's will. Galatians 3:19

■ **Why do we take communion?**

Then he broke the bread and said, "This is my body; it is for you. Do this to remember me." In the same way, after they ate, Jesus took the cup. He said, "This cup is the new agreement that is sealed with the blood of my death. When you drink this, do it to remember me." I Corinthians 11:24, 25

■ **How would you describe God?**

He is holy and wonderful. Psalm 111:9

■ **What emotion gives the devil a foothold in your life?**

Don't let the sun go down with you still angry—get over it quickly; for when you are angry you give a mighty foothold to the devil. Ephesians 4:26, 27 TLB

■ **For what great purpose did the Son of God come to earth?**

The Son of God came for this purpose: to destroy the devil's work. I John 3:8

Do you need to destroy some work the devil is doing in your life? Call on the Son of God.

■ **Jesus was Jewish so why do most Christians go to church on Sunday rather than on the Jewish Sabbath (Saturday)?**

The day after the Sabbath day was the first day of the week. The angel said to the woman, "Don't be afraid. I know that you are looking for Jesus, who has been crucified. He is not here. He has risen from the dead as he said he would." Matthew 28:1, 5

It's in honor of Jesus rising from the dead on Sunday morning.

■ **What is a four word phrase to keep you out of trouble at home?**

Do everything in love. I Corinthians 16:14

■ **One thing people want is to be happy—I'll say, "Amen" to that but the question is, "How do you obtain lasting happiness?" Erroneously many think money creates happiness. That's probably true for brief periods; but where does real happiness come from?**

But Jesus said, ". . . happy are those who hear the teaching of God and obey it." Luke 11:28

I can testify that Jesus' formula works. Happiness just doesn't come out of Rocky Mountain polluted thin air (I live in the Denver area). You have to work at it. Sorry to use a four letter word—WORK—but for most promises in the Bible there are conditions that go along with them. In this instance the promise is happiness, but the condition is you must "hear the teaching of God and obey it." This means an effort on your part. So how do you "hear the teaching of God?" The best way is to read your Bible regularly. Turn on the radio and tune in a Christian station and go to a good church where they teach from the Scriptures.

■ **Has this thought ever bothered you? "What if, upon my death, there is a mix-up in the paperwork and I find myself trying to explain to someone that I don't belong in hell."**

The Spirit is God's proof that you belong to him. God gave you the Spirit to show that God will make you free when the final day comes. Ephesians 4:30

Don't worry, God the Holy Spirit is keeping track of who the real Christians are.

■ **What does the Holy Bible say about cremation?**

So Moses, the disciple of the Lord, died in the land of Moab as the Lord had said. The Lord buried him in a valley near Beth-Peor in Moab, but no one knows the exact place. Deuteronomy 34:5, 6 TLB

The Bible says nothing about cremation, it only talks about burial.

■ **Is Jesus in the Old Testament?**

My strength is gone, like water poured out onto the ground, and my bones are out of joint. My heart is like wax; it has melted inside me. My strength has dried up like a clay pot, and my tongue sticks to the top of my mouth. You laid me in the dust of death. Evil people have surrounded me; like dogs they have trapped me. They have bitten my arms and legs. I can count all my bones; people look and stare at me. They divided my clothes among them, and they threw lots for my clothing. Psalm 22:14-18

In Psalm 22 it describes Jesus being crucified. That is very enlightening because at the time the Psalm was written the state punishment in Israel was stoning. Crucifixion was invented by the Romans but that was 700 years after this Psalm was written!

Prophecy is history written in advance. It alone proves the Bible is divine and not written from man's mind. God's signature is Bible prophecy.

■ **How do you obtain spiritual strength in the midst of your troubles?**

God will strengthen you with his own great power so that you will not give up when troubles come, but you will be patient. Colossians 1:11

■ **If God, using his infinite wisdom, put in a book the formula for a happy and satisfying life, wouldn't you read it?**

Your love must be real. Hate what is evil, and hold on to what is good. Love each other like brothers and sisters. Give each other more honor than you want for yourselves. Do not be lazy but work hard, serving the Lord with all your heart. Be joyful because you have hope. Be patient when trouble comes, and pray at all times. Share with God's people who need help. Bring strangers in need into your homes. Wish good for those who harm you; wish them well and do not curse them. Be happy with those who are happy, and be sad with those who are sad. Live in peace with each other. Do not be proud, but make friends with those who seem unimportant. Do not think how smart you are. If someone does wrong to you, do not pay him back by doing wrong to him. Try to do what everyone thinks is right. Do your best to live in peace with everyone. My friends, do not try to punish others when they wrong you, but wait for God to punish them with his anger. It is written: "I will punish those who do wrong; I will repay them," says the Lord. But you should do this: If your enemy is hungry, feed him; if he is thirsty, give him a drink. Doing this will be like pouring burning coals on his head. Romans 12:9-20

■ **Are you special to God?**

All the days planned for me were written in your book before I was one day old. Psalm 139:16

The circumstances of your birth may not be what you think they should have been. However, God planned your life long before the word mistake came along! Rejoice in your life.

■ What is the purpose of stars and planets?

The heavens tell the glory of God, and the skies announce what his hands have made.   Psalm 19:1

Because God's universe is so incredible would it surprise you to know that 90% of astronomers believe in God?[1]

■ In a marriage, who should submit to whom?

Yield [wives and husbands] to obey each other because you respect Christ.   Ephesians 5:21

■ Even though you submit to each other, can the wife wear the pants in the family?

As the church yields to Christ, so you wives should yield to your husbands in everything.   Ephesians 5:24

I didn't write the answer—no letters please.

■ We just read what the wife should do, but what is the husband's responsibility?

In the same way, husbands should love their wives as they love their own bodies.   Ephesians 5:28

■ What does God want for you in Christ Jesus?

Always be joyful. Pray continually, and give thanks whatever happens. That is what God wants for you in Christ Jesus.   I Thessalonians 5:16-18

■ Are you aware that when you do bad things they are written down and recorded in heavenly books?

And I saw the dead, great and small, standing before the throne. Then books were opened, and the book of life was opened. The dead were judged by what they had done, which was written in the books. Revelation 20:12

Be glad this verse is referring to unsaved people. When you accept Jesus Christ as your Savior, the things written down against you are completely covered over by the blood from the Cross of Jesus.

■ **How far is the east from the west?**

He has taken our sins away from us as far as the east is from west. Psalm 103:12

It's an endless distance, so if you have asked God to forgive your sins, that is how far they have been taken away. The forgiven sins are no longer in the books. Therefore they cannot be judged. Now would be a good time to say, hallelujah!

■ **You don't have to be a rocket scientist to answer this like an expert if you know your Bible. What holds the universe together?**

He was before all else began and it is his [God's] power that holds everything together. Colossians 1:17 TLB

■ **What is the prime risk of having too much material wealth?**

"If I have too much, I might reject you and say, 'I don't know the LORD.' " Proverbs 30:9

■ **Does the Lord hear you when you ask for His help?**

Surely the LORD'S power is enough to save you. He can hear you when you ask him for help. Isaiah 59:1

■ **What is it that separates people from God?**

It is your evil that has separated you from your God. Your sins cause him to turn away from you. Isaiah 59:2

■ **With whom is God pleased?**

These are the people I [God] am pleased with: those who are not proud or stubborn and who fear my word. Isaiah 66:2

■ **Can discovering what's in God's Bible blow you away?**

"The wind blows where it wants to and you hear the sound of it, but you don't know where the wind comes from or where it is going." John 3:8

The answer is yes, and people from North Dakota and Wyoming can relate well to this Scripture.

■ **What is the most popular verse in the entire Bible?**

"God loved the world so much that He gave his one and only Son so that whoever believes in him may not be lost, but have eternal life." John 3:16

A good friend saved my life during a rafting trip. Thanks again, Dave. Now it's my turn.

■ **If you tell someone about Jesus and they decide to accept Him as their Savior, did you get that person saved?**

"Then who can be saved?" Jesus looked at them and said, "This is something people cannot do, but God can." Mark 10:26, 27

Our job is to witness. It is the Holy Spirit who does the saving.

■ **Is there anyone greater than Jesus?**

"The One [Jesus] who comes from above is greater than all." John 3:31

■ **Are you suffering? Are you hurting? Are you miserable? I feel for you, but if you believe in God's Son for your salvation look what's ahead for you.**

The sufferings we have now are nothing compared to the great glory that will be shown to us. Romans 8:18

■ **Get this down in your spirit and it should raise your joy level. When does eternal life begin?**

"I tell you the truth, whoever hears what I say and believes in the One who sent me has eternal life. That person will not be judged guilty but has already left death and entered life." John 5:24

Eternal life begins the moment you believe Jesus died for your sins and you ask for forgiveness.

■ This brings up a good point that should vitalize your joy. If, according to John 5:24 death has already left, do you ever really die? Your body stops functioning and dies but the real you, your soul, never dies! The soul is the real you because it consists of your mind, emotions, and will. Now your question might be, "OK Myron (That's the real me. It's the name on my birth certificate.), show me a Scripture that proves my soul doesn't die." You asked for one, I'll give you three.

"I tell you the truth, whoever obeys my teaching will never die." John 8:51

Jesus said to her, "I am the resurrection and the life. Those who believe in me will have life even if they die. And everyone who lives and believes in me will never die." John 11:25, 26

We are confident, yes, well pleased rather to be absent from the body and to be present with the Lord. II Corinthians 5:8 NKJV

Now this saying should begin to make logical sense. If you're born once, you will die twice. But if you're born twice, you will die once. I was going to explain this, but I thought if you didn't fully understand, it would entice you to keep reading.

■ The Ten Commandments are found in Exodus, chapter 20. Incredibly they are no longer found on the classroom wall! They are not numbered 1 through 10 but see if you can find each one in your Bible. It's not as easy as you might think.

Occasionally I am going to ask you to get actively involved. Your response may be to skip the venture. My hope is that you not only become familiar about the Scriptures, but that you become involved with the Book itself by looking up a few of the answers.

■ **What does the Bible say about drinking wine? We have all heard from the Scriptures that a little wine is good for the stomach. So if a little is good, why not have more?**

Do not be drunk with wine, which will ruin you, but be filled with the Spirit. Ephesians 5:18

■ **What is the formula for receiving respect and pleasing God? Please notice what it says about your clothes, car, house, education, job, amount of money you make, and how much you do for God.**

Don't ever forget kindness and truth. Wear them like a necklace. Write them on your heart as if on a tablet. Then you will be respected and will please both God and people. Proverbs 3:3, 4

■ **Is the formula for success so simple that everyone can be successful?**

Remember the LORD in all you do, and he will give you success. Proverbs 3:6

■ **Sometimes it seems like the whole world is on the verge of being out of control. Does anyone have a handle on the situation?**

God has put Christ over all rulers, authorities, powers, and kings, not only in this world but also in the next. Ephesians 1:21

■ **We have heard we are to fear the Lord. That word is better translated to mean respect. We shouldn't fear someone who loves us. Should we?**

In Christ we can come before God with freedom and without fear. Christ's love is greater than anyone can ever know, but I pray that you will be able to know that love. Then you can be filled with the fullness of God. Ephesians 3:12, 19

■ **The Holy Spirit produces fruit. Can you name some of this divine produce?**

But the Spirit produces the fruit of love, joy, peace, patience, kindness, goodness, faithfulness, gentleness, self-control. Galatians 5:22

■ **Once a person has accepted Jesus as their Savior they have a new life in Christ. Where does that new life come from?**

We get our new life from the Spirit, so we should follow the Spirit. Galatians 5:25

■ **If you are not a Christian and you saw a miracle from God, would you change your life and believe in Jesus?**

Then Jesus criticized the cities where he did most of his miracles, because the people did not change their lives and stop sinning. Matthew 11:20

Seeing a miracle would get your attention, but believing in Jesus comes through faith.

So faith comes from hearing the Good News, and people hear the Good News when someone tells them about Christ. Romans 10:17

■ **There is quite a number of gods if you add them up from all the different religions. But how many of them can save your soul?**

"I, the LORD, have been your God since you were in the land of Egypt. You should have known no other God except me. I am the only one who saves." Hosea 13:4

■ **I am a firm believer that we are living in the time of Christ's second coming. Will Jesus' coming surprise us? Will He come like a thief in the night? If Christians have their eyes and ears open can we know the season of his return?**

Before the Lord GOD does anything, he tells his plans to his servants, the prophets. Amos 3:7

Today God reveals, through His Word and His people, the things He has in store for us. Tune your eyes and ears to the Scriptures and end time messages to be aware of the season of Christ's return.

■ **Can we know what God is thinking?**

He is the one who makes the mountains and creates the wind and makes his thoughts known to people.   Amos 4:13

God's thoughts are close to you—where is that Bible anyway?

■ **God is love. In His eyes is it OK to hate anything?**

Hate evil and love good.   Amos 5:15

■ **When is it OK not to tell the truth?**

Don't use your mouth to tell lies; don't ever say things that are not true. Proverbs 4:24

As a Christian, what would you do if some scumbag wanted to know where an innocent loved one was for the purpose of killing him? Ron Rhodes, President of Reasoning from the Scriptures Ministries has an excellent answer. ". . . there are Scriptures which indicate that under certain circumstances, lying is not condemned. For example, though the Hebrew midwives were commanded by the Egyptian Pharaoh to let newborn baby boys die, the midwives disobeyed the Pharaoh and lied to him when questioned about it (Exodus 1:15-19).   To the Hebrew midwives . . . lifesaving was higher on the ethical scale than truthtelling. God not only did not condemn the midwives for lying, He was kind to them for their merciful act.

"A more recent example would be the numerous Christians who lied to the Nazis in order to protect Jews from being captured and exterminated. In such cases lying is permissible because lifesaving is a higher ethic than truthtelling."

■ **What road should the Christian travel everyday?**

Don't turn off the road of goodness . . . . Proverbs 4:27

■ **You might be living on your land, but who really owns it? You, the bank, or God?**

" 'The land really belongs to me [GOD], so you can't sell it for all time. You are only foreigners and travelers living for a while on my land.' " Leviticus 25:23

■ **If you are left-handed, like me, there must be something special about it because it was purposefully mentioned in the Scriptures.**

When the people cried to the LORD, he sent someone to save them. He was Ehud, son of Gera, from the people of Benjamin, who was left-handed. Judges 3:15

■ **Where did Samson get his great strength?**

Then the Spirit of the LORD entered Samson and gave him great power. Judges 15:14

■ **What does the Lord look at when He looks at you?**

"People look at the outside of a person, but the LORD looks at the heart." I Samuel 16:7

Chapter Two

"I believe the Bible is the best gift God has ever given to man."
- Abraham Lincoln -

■ **How much is wisdom worth?**

Wisdom is worth more than silver; it brings more profit than gold. Wisdom is more precious than rubies; nothing you could want is equal to it. Proverbs 3:14, 15

■ **Wisdom is very valuable, but if you know the right person can you have it free for the asking?**

But if any of you needs wisdom, you should ask God for it. He is generous and enjoys giving to all people, so he will give you wisdom. James 1:5

■ **Can God's Word make a common person wise?**

The rules of the LORD can be trusted; they make plain people wise. Psalm 19:7

■ **Who was the wisest person on earth? He used Godly wisdom and wrote most of the Proverbs.**

God gave Solomon great wisdom so he could understand many things . . . . . He was wiser than anyone on earth. I Kings 4:29, 31

■ **I hate to bring it up but is this next verse talking about the lack of exercise, eating, smoking and drinking habits?**

Wise people's lives get better and better. They avoid whatever would cause their death. Proverbs 15:24

This may not be conventional, but I feel pressed to get personal and the subject does apply to many. Kim Bob, your dad died of cancer and you quit smoking because of that. Now you are smoking again and you asked me to pray for you. I did. Now it's your turn to make the next wise move.

Paul Harvey reported that smokers puff an average of fifteen years off their lives!

■ **What purpose did it serve when the Israelites sacrificed animals on the altar?**

With the goats' blood they made an offering on the altar to remove the sins of the Israelites so they would belong to God. II Chronicles 29:24

■ **Why don't Christians sacrifice animals for their sins?**

So through Christ we will surely be saved from God's anger, because we have been made right with God by the blood of Christ's death. Romans 5:9

Jesus was the final sacrifice for all sin. No other blood sacrifice is required. Jesus paid it all for past, present, and future sin.

■ **What would it take to make God angry with you?**

But Hezekiah did not thank God for his kindness, because he was so proud. So the LORD was angry with him . . . . II Chronicles 32:25

■ **When will the Lord call you His friend?**

The LORD hates those who do wrong, but he is a friend to those who are honest. Proverbs 3:32

■ **How can another man's wife cost you your life?**

... and a woman who takes part in adultery may cost you your life. Proverbs 6:26

■ **What is the only door you can go through and find salvation on the other side?**

So Jesus said, ". . . I am the door, and the person who enters through me will be saved . . . ." John 10:7, 9

■ **Were the six days of creation 24 hour days or long extended periods of time? Take things in the Bible to be literal unless the text lets you know otherwise. In the previous item it is obvious Jesus is not a literal door. Sal Giardina, scientist, reported on a gentleman who wrote to some of the most outstanding Hebrew scholars at world class universities asking them to translate the Hebrew word for day as found in Genesis, Chapter 1. They all unanimously replied that the word should be translated to be commonly understood as a 24-hour period.**

Work and get everything done during six days each week, but the seventh day is a day of rest to honor the LORD your God . . . . The reason is that in six days the LORD made everything—the sky, the earth, the sea, and everything in them. On the seventh day he rested. Exodus 20:9, 11

If you don't agree with literal days, how do you explain Genesis 2:3? It states, "God blessed the seventh day and made it a holy day . . . ." The Sabbath day is not an extended period of time, it is just 24 hours long.

■ **Angels are a creation of God, but when were they created?**

The Bible doesn't address some things and this is one of them.

■ **What senseless act, besides war and too much alcohol, destroys people?**

A man who takes part in adultery has no sense; he will destroy himself. Proverbs 6:32

I modified this to include alcohol because a friend of mine just died of cirrhosis of the liver. That only took about twenty-five years off his life!

■ **Why concentrate so heavily on having a lot of wealth when at death it will be meaningless to you?   Wouldn't it be wise to concentrate on the Word of God that can save you from death?**

Riches will not help when it's time to die, but right living will save you from death. Proverbs 11:4

Death here refers to a persons second death or going to hell.   The second death is explained later.

■ **Many people wish they could win a sweepstakes or the lottery. Have you watched a program or read about these "lucky people" and seen how many of their lives become all messed up after "winning big"? Solomon's words are very wise.**

It is better to be poor and respect the LORD than to be wealthy and have much trouble. Proverbs 15:16

■ **What are your thoughts on predestination? Some people believe God created certain people to go to hell. I'm glad I don't serve a God like that. Aren't you?**

But God is being patient with you. He does not want anyone to be lost, but he wants all people to change their hearts and lives. II Peter 3:9

■ **What kind of worth would you put on your favorite possessions if they were going to burn up and no insurance money would be paid?**

. . . and the earth and everything in it will be burned up. In that way everything will be destroyed. So what kind of people should you be? You should live holy lives and serve God, as you wait for and look forward to the coming of the day of God. II Peter 3:10-12

■ **Is the present heaven and earth going to exist forever?**

But God made a promise to us, and we are waiting for a new heaven and a new earth where goodness lives. II Peter 3:13

It is after the earth is burned up that God creates a new earth for His people.

■ **If you could ask God for just one thing that lasts forever what would it be?**

And now we announce to you that he has life that continues forever. I John 1:2

This is a very serious answer but the way it reads it almost sounds like it just came over the loud speaker at a discount store. Allow me to paraphrase the way you might hear it at Wal-Mart. "The Eternal Department Manager has just announced an Easter special. He offers life that continues forever for a limited time. Cost has been paid in full by the Manager this one time only. Don't miss out on this truly wonderful bargain."

■ **When reading Scripture what emotion should you experience?**

We write this to you so you can be full of joy with us. I John 1:4

■ **What is one way to tell if you are a Christian in name only or if you are a true born again Christian?**

So if we say we have fellowship with God, but we continue living in darkness [sin], we are liars and do not follow the truth. I John 1:6

■ **Is it possible to live life without ever sinning?**

If we say we have not sinned, we make God a liar, and we do not accept God's teaching. I John 1:10

■ **Can a pastor or priest take away your sin?**

But if anyone does sin, we have a helper in the presence of the Father—Jesus Christ, the One who does what is right. He is the way our sins are taken away, and not only our sins but the sins of all people. I John 2:1, 2

■ **Who is the only one to take away sin?** This question is very basic and even simplistic but believe it or not some churches get this one wrong. That's why it is so important to know what is in your Bible. The next time someone says to you, "I forgive your sins," you can quote I John 2:12 to them.

I write to you, dear children, because your sins are forgiven through Christ. I John 2:12

■ **Can you get to heaven by believing in God the Father only?**

Whoever does not accept the Son [Jesus Christ] does not have the Father. But whoever confesses the Son has the Father too. I John 2:23

With important questions like this I want to be sure you answered correctly. It's no.

■ **The first time you stand before God, will you have fear and be ashamed?**

. . . my dear children, live in him so that when Christ comes back, we can be without fear and not be ashamed in his presence. I John 2:28

How do you "live in him?" As a believer stay near to God. Ask for forgiveness, study His Word and be in fellowship with God's people.

■ **How should you live?**

So I tell you: Live by following the Spirit. Then you will not do what your sinful selves want. Our sinful selves want what is against the Spirit, and the Spirit wants what is against our sinful selves. The two are against each other, so you cannot do just what you please. Galatians 5:16, 17

■ **What must you do to keep out of heaven?**

The wrong things the sinful self does are clear: being sexually unfaithful, not being pure, taking part in sexual sins, worshipping gods, doing witchcraft, hating, making trouble, being jealous, being angry, being selfish, making people angry with each other, causing divisions among people, feeling envy, being drunk, having wild and wasteful parties, and doing other things like these. I warn you now as I warned you before: Those who do these things will not inherit God's kingdom. Galatians 5:19-21

The only way these things can keep you out of heaven is if you have never been forgiven for them. A Christian has been forgiven for all sins, but has a responsibility to abstain from committing the same sin over and over again. After reading that verse do you think a married politician in Washington can have oral sex with another woman and still think it would be acceptable to God? It isn't to the God of the Bible.

■ **What is the simplest definition of sin?**

Yes, sin is living against God's law. I John 3:4

■ **Is there another choice for people besides being under God's grace or His wrath?**

Those who believe in the Son have eternal life, but those who do not obey the Son will never have life. God's anger stays on them. John 3:36

■ **What simple thing must you do to be like Christ?**

Christ is all that is right. So to be like Christ a person must do what is right. I John 3:7

■ **Cain (one of the first sons of Adam and Eve) was just like the devil. How did he treat his brother?**

Do not be like Cain who belonged to the Evil One and killed his brother. I John 3:12

■ **Who was the first astronaut? I'll give you a clue—it wasn't a Russian or Alan Shepard.**

It was by faith that Enoch was taken to heaven so he would not die. He could not be found, because God had taken him away. Hebrews 11:5

■ **Crossing the Red Sea on dry ground is a famous Bible story, but how many know the Jordan River stopped flowing so the Israelites could cross over into the Promised Land?**

During harvest the Jordan overflows its banks. When the priests carrying the Ark came to the edge of the river and stepped into the water, the water upstream stopped flowing. Joshua 3:15, 16

There is a lesson on faith in this passage. God promised that the water would stop flowing, but the priests had to step out in faith and make the first move. It would be nice to have our prayers answered without us doing anything, but usually God wants us to participate; and normally it's by taking the first step.

■ **True or False? People consider they have failed if they haven't been able to get their friends or relatives saved.**

"You will be my witnesses—in Jerusalem, in all Judea, in Samaria, and in every part of the world." Acts 1:8

It is the Holy Spirit's job to do the actual saving. Your job is to witness.

■ **John Loeffler, host of the radio program, The Missler Report, said, with tongue-in-cheek, about the big bang theory, "First there was nothing, then it exploded." Sal Giardina, scientist, says, "You have to believe in either eternal dirt or eternal God." With profound statements like that, isn't it logical to believe in God?**

If you use your mouth to say, "Jesus is Lord," and if you believe in your heart that God raised Jesus from the dead, you will be saved. Romans 10:9

■ **Is it OK for a Christian to drink alcohol? It might not be a sin for you, but I think we should follow the example of John the Baptist. Even before he was born it was prophesied that he was to be a great man for the Lord. And then the very next sentence in that prophecy says wine or beer would never touch his lips. I think the very fact these two things were mentioned together is telling Christians that drinking is not looked upon with favor from the Lord.**

John will be a great man for the Lord. He will never drink wine or beer, and even from birth, he will be filled with the Holy Spirit. Luke 1:15

■ **If the need arises can an angel talk to you?**

But the angel said to him, "Zechariah, don't be afraid. God has heard your prayer. Luke 1:13

■ **Is the main job of an angel being a messenger for God?**

The angel answered him, "I am Gabriel. I stand before God who sent me to talk to you and tell you this good news." Luke 1:19

The word angel actually means messenger of God.

■ **Are there examples in Scripture of people going to heaven and then returning to tell about it?**

I know a man in Christ who was taken up to the third heaven fourteen years ago. I do not know whether the man was in his body or out of his body, but God knows. And I know that this man was taken up to paradise. II Corinthians 12:2-4

*Be careful which books you read on near death experiences. The majority of authors say most, if not all people, have good experiences. The Scriptures in Matthew, chapter 7, proclaims only a few people make it to heaven. A credible author in this area is Dr. Maurice Rawlings, M.D. His books are **Beyond Death's Door** and **To Hell and Back.** These books are extremely enlightening.*

■ **I just love end time Bible prophecy so my ears really perked up when I heard Dr. Richard Eby, physician and author, speak. He said that Jesus told him he would not die before He would come to take His people to heaven in the Rapture. This man is over 85 years old. I have met and talked with him, read his books, seen him on TV many times and believe he is credible. In light of these next Scriptures, judge for yourself if it sounds too unbelievable. Does our redemption draw nigh?**

Simeon had been told by the Holy Spirit that he would not die before he saw the Christ promised by the Lord. Luke 2:26

Mary and Joseph brought the baby Jesus to the Temple . . . Simeon took the baby in his arms and thanked God . . . . Luke 2:27-28

■ Is it true some people will never die physically?

And those who have died believing in Christ will rise first. After that, we who are still alive will be gathered up [raptured] with them in the clouds to meet the Lord in the air. And we will be with the Lord forever. So encourage each other with these words. I Thessalonians 4:16-18

We are living in the last of the last days and I believe we are that generation of believers who will not taste death. If you are born again and alive at the time of the Rapture, you will never die! The word Rapture in Christian terminology means to be caught up (gathered up). It occurs at an unknown day and hour, in the twinkling of an eye, when Jesus calls all true living Christians home to heaven. It is an imminent event, meaning it could happen at any moment. If you have not trusted Jesus as your Savior (been born again, saved) you will be left on earth to go through the horrifying Tribulation period.

■ In eternity, where are you going to live and what are you going to be doing?

" . . . and they [God's holy people] will rule on the earth." Revelation 5:10

Prior to the soon coming seven year Tribulation period Christians are raptured to heaven. At the end of the Tribulation we return with Jesus and watch as He defeats the Antichrist in the battle of Armageddon. We will then rule and reign with Christ for one thousand years here on a peaceful earth. During this Millennium Satan will be bound in hell. At the end of that time the devil will be set free for a short period to recruit and deceive the mortal human beings we have been ruling over. With his new recruits Satan will try unsuccessfully to battle God. After the battle, God will cast Satan into the lake of fire forever. At the end of the Millennium is where time ends and eternity begins. God then creates new heavens and a new earth. The new Jerusalem, the city in which Christians will live forever, comes down from heaven to the new earth where we will rule and reign forever with Christ. Maybe ruling and reigning doesn't sound like as much fun as Saturday night bowling, but just trust God it will be the most enjoyable fun time you can imagine.

Then I saw a new heaven and a new earth. The first heaven and the first earth had disappeared, and there was no sea anymore. And I saw the holy city, the new Jerusalem, coming down out of heaven from God. It was prepared like a bride dressed for her husband. And I heard a loud voice from the throne, saying, "Now God's presence is with people, and he will live with them, and they will be his people. God himself will be with them and will be their God." Revelation 21:1-3

■ **Can we know when the Rapture is getting close or is that forbidden knowledge?**

But you, brothers and sisters [Christians], are not living in darkness, and so that day [the Rapture] will not surprise you like a thief. I Thessalonians 5:4

People become very skeptical when there is talk about how close the Rapture and the Second Coming of Jesus is. That probably comes from these Bible statements. "Nobody will know the day and hour" and "He will come like a thief in the night." I agree that we can't know the day, but we can know the season. The people caught unaware as when a thief strikes are those who are not looking for His return. Please don't be skeptical, but check out for yourself the signs that point to His soon return.

■ **I get exuberant talking about end-time prophecy. Have I gone off the deep end or is prophecy important?**

Do not treat prophecy as if it were unimportant. I Thessalonians 5:20

Twenty-seven percent of Bible verses deal with events that happen in the future from the time they were written (Bible prophecy). If almost one third of the total number of verses focus on a particular theme it must be very significant and worthy of some of your study time. Dr. Tim

LaHaye, author, stated, "The second most repeated subject in the Bible is the Second Coming of Christ."

■ **What would you say if I said I could guarantee that these are the last days? Maybe it's good I can't hear your remarks. Out of the 6000 years of human history the 2000 years since Jesus' birth is the Church Age or the last days. I believe we are within a few years of the end of the last days, but I can't guarantee that.**

My dear children, these are the last days. You have heard that the enemy of Christ is coming, and now many enemies of Christ are already here. This is how we know that these are the last days. I John 2:18

■ **Going from B.C. to A.D., was there a year zero? No. There was 1 B.C. and A.D. 1. Some are probably wondering if 6000 years of man's history is accurate. From history we see Moses at about 1500 B.C., Abraham at 2000 B.C., Noah at about 3000 B.C., and Adam & Eve at 4000 B.C. From Jesus' birth to the present is 2000 years. 4000 B.C. plus A.D. 2000 equals Jesus is coming soon!**

A.D. comes from the Latin words anno domini and means, "In the year of our Lord." For our dating system to use Jesus' birth as its basis should tell us that Jesus was more than just a "great teacher." Ironically, for those who believe He was just a great teacher, He did not teach us to date world history by using His birth as a starting point!

■ **What is the main message of the entire Bible?**

For You [Jesus] were slain, and have redeemed us to God by Your blood. Revelation 5:9 NKJV

The blessed answer is redemption (bought back—Jesus paid for our sins with His blood).

■ **Who hears from God? The longer I've been a Christian the deeper my insights become into the things of God. One thing I've figured out is people who hear from God are the ones that talk to Him regularly and read His Word often. If you think you are doing pretty well at praying, reading the Bible and going to church, check out this godly lady.**

Then her husband died, and she was a widow for eighty-four years. Anna never left the Temple but worshipped God, going without food and praying day and night. Luke 2:37

■ **Should we fret over gray hairs, Stephen?**

Gray hair is like a crown of honor; it is earned by living a good life. Proverbs 16:31

It's OK to fret, but just a little.

■ **How do you tell when someone is a true friend or a reliable relative?**

A friend loves you all the time, and a brother helps in time of trouble. Proverbs 17:17

■ **Is it OK to be a co-signer on a loan?**

It is not wise to promise to pay what your neighbor owes. Proverbs 17:18

■ **Why drink alcohol when the Scriptures say this about it?**

Later it [alcohol] bites like a snake with poison in its fangs. Who has trouble? Who has pain? Who fights? Who complains? Who has unnecessary bruises? Who has bloodshot eyes? It is people who drink too much wine, who try out all different kinds of strong drinks. Proverbs 23:32, 29, 30

■ **What was the first miracle Jesus performed?**

So they took the water to the master. When he tasted it, the water had become wine. So in Cana of Galilee Jesus did his first miracle. There he showed his glory, and his followers believed in him. John 2:8, 9, 11

There are many Scriptures that warn how dangerous strong drink is and Scripture says point blank that if you are a drunkard you can't enter heaven. So why did Jesus make wine for his first miracle? I have two insights that might shed some light on this: First, I've heard that grape juice in those days was called wine. Secondly, wine, I understand, in Bible times was made 1/11th as strong as it is today.

■ **Why are Christians bothered by trouble? The reasons vary, but take heart God has promised they will not totally overwhelm you.**

Even though good people may be bothered by trouble seven times, they are never defeated, but the wicked are overwhelmed by trouble. Proverbs 24:16

■ **Don't you get tired of people talking about all their wonderful accomplishments?**

It is not good to eat too much honey, nor does it bring you honor to brag about yourself. Proverbs 25:27

■ **If you don't live by the golden rule is there a good chance your deeds will backfire on you?**

Whoever digs a pit for others will fall into it. Whoever tries to roll a boulder down on others will be crushed by it. Proverbs 26:27

If someone is doing you dirty, just keep doing what is right. Have patience and see if this proverb doesn't hold true for the guilty party.

■ **I say war is next to the dumbest thing on planet earth. Will there be a glad day when there is no more war?**

Then [beginning of Millennium] they will make their swords into plows and their spears into hooks for trimming trees. Nations will no longer fight other nations, nor will they train for war anymore. Isaiah 2:4

Just in case you were wondering, the dumbest thing on this planet is to miss heaven.

■ **Who is good every day? Who does no wrong? Who can be trusted every day? Who governs fairly each morning?**

But the LORD is good, and he is there in that city. He does no wrong. Every morning he governs the people fairly; every day he can be trusted. Zephaniah 3:5

■ **Why should we honor and respect God?**

The LORD All-Powerful says, "A child honors his father, and a servant honors his master. I am a father, so why don't you honor me? I am a master, so why don't you respect me? Malachi 1:6

Give honor and respect because God is Father and Master.

■ **Can a person do anything so bad that God won't accept him back?**

"Return to me, and I will return to you," says the LORD All-Powerful. Malachi 3:7

The good answer is no.

■ **Does God change?**

"I the LORD do not change" Malachi 3:6

■ **Do certain salespeople, telemarketers, leeches or some religious people who show up at your door in pairs have your best interest in mind?**

It is good for people to show interest in you, but only if their purpose is good. Galatians 4:18

These religious people I am referring to are in false religions. They certainly do not have your best interest in mind, and there is more discussion of them later.

■ **Did someone have to shed their blood so your sins could be forgiven?**

In Christ we are set free by the blood of his death, and so we have forgiveness of sins. Ephesians 1:7

■ **When did God decide to send Jesus to earth as a sacrifice for your sin?**

In Christ we were chosen to be God's people, because from the very beginning God had decided this in keeping with his plan. Ephesians 1:11

■ **If you are a believer in Christ, what mark of ownership proves you belong to God?**

And in Christ, God put his special mark of ownership on you by giving you the Holy Spirit that he had promised. Ephesians 1:13

■ **Do you want a statement of something to get excited about? God has promised you rich and glorious blessings!**

. . . so you will know the hope to which he has called us and that you will know how rich and glorious are the blessings God has promised his holy people. Ephesians 1:18

That verse should arouse your interest to dig into the Bible to discover your hope and to find out what the rich and glorious blessings are God has promised to YOU.

■ **Where do the evil spirits gather to plot against us?**

. . . following the ruler of the evil powers that are above the earth. Ephesians 2:2

■ **How is it possible for you to even have the opportunity to be saved?**

You have been saved by God's grace. Ephesians 2:5

A good explanation of grace is:
> **G** *od's*
> **R** *iches*
> **A** *t*
> **C** *hrist's*
> **E** *xpense*

■ Can you count on someone else witnessing to your friends and relatives about Jesus being the only way to heaven? Are there a lot of individuals helping people get to heaven, or just a few?

Jesus said to his followers, "There are many people to harvest but only a few workers to help harvest them. Pray to the Lord, who owns the harvest, that he will send more workers to gather his harvest." Matthew 9:37, 38

Good news! I have written a 12-page booklet that can help you witness. It is a road map to heaven and consists of short, convincing statements like this, "If there were more than one way to get to heaven, wouldn't there be more than just Jesus Christ's name used as a swear word?" Information about the booklet is under Suggested Reading at the end of this book.

■ As astounding as it sounds, many who attend church can't give the correct answer to how a person gets into heaven! What is the most incorrect answer given when people are asked, "Why should God let you into heaven?"
   a. I've been good.
   b. I am a good person.
   c. Basically I have been a good person.
   d. All the above.

If you use your mouth to say, "Jesus is Lord," and if you believe in your heart that God raised Jesus from the dead, you will be saved. Romans 10:9

Can a person get into heaven by being good? I am trying to make some of these real easy so if you didn't answer a resounding NO you have to go to the blackboard and write this item out ten times.

■ Does God really know how many hairs are on your head?

God even knows how many hairs are on your head. Matthew 10:30

■ Who is going to be considered great in heaven? Maybe it's you.

The greatest person in the kingdom of heaven is the one who makes himself humble . . . . Matthew 18:4

■ **How many times must you forgive a fellow believer?**

Then Peter came to him and asked, "Sir, how often should I forgive a brother who sins against me? Seven times?" "No!" Jesus replied, "seventy times seven!" Matthew 18:22 TLB

Does that mean you keep a count? No, it means you must forgive each time. Notice it doesn't say to forgive only when the other person comes crawling back or if they ask for it.

■ **What is the entire duty of people?**

Honor God and obey his commands, because this is all people must do. Ecclesiastes 12:13

■ **Is a baby in the womb human or just cells?**

You don't know where the wind will blow, and you don't know how a baby grows inside the mother. Ecclesiastes 11:5

In God's infinite wisdom, He called it a baby.

These six things the LORD hates ... hands that shed innocent blood ... Proverbs 6:16, 17 NKJV

■ **Do you get your self-worth from:**
    a. What others say about you?
    b. What you think about yourself?
    c. What God says about you?

Two sparrows cost only a penny, but not even one of them can die without your Father's knowing it. God even knows how many hairs are on your head. So don't be afraid. You are worth much more than many sparrows. Matthew 10:29, 30

■ **Who are the truly happy people?**

But the truly happy people are those who carefully study God's perfect law [the Bible] that makes people free, and they continue to study it. They do not forget what they heard, but they obey what God's teaching says. Those who do this will be made happy. James 1:25

■ **What does God want for you?**

Always be joyful . . . . That is what God wants for you in Christ Jesus. I Thessalonians 5:16, 17

■ **Can you trust what TV evangelists, your pastor, or I say about the Scriptures?**

The Bereans were eager to hear what Paul and Silas said and studied the Scriptures every day to find out if these things were true. Acts 17:11

Many people can be trusted although it is of utmost importance you check out what people say and compare it against Scripture. False churches and cults would be virtually void of people if the members followed the wisdom of the Bereans!

■ **Is money the root of all evil? YES! To solve this problem send all your money to Mike and Linda, PO Box 0, Just Kidding, USA. When people quote this next Scripture incorrectly what important word is left out?**

The love [emphasis added] of money causes all kinds of evil. I Timothy 6:10

The keyword of why that was a false statement—the love of money.

■ **Where did the idea come from to pray and give thanks before meals?**

. . . foods which God created to be eaten with thanks . . . . I Timothy 4:3

■ **How about those pay backs people deserve? When is it OK to get even?**

Be sure that no one pays back wrong for wrong, but always try to do what is good for each other and for all people. I Thessalonians 5:15

■ **Can you be rich, yet have no money?**

Serving God does make us very rich, if we are satisfied with what we have. I Timothy 6:6

■ **Is it true that all Scripture is given by God?**

All Scripture is given by God and is useful for teaching, for showing people what is wrong in their lives, for correcting faults, and for teaching how to live right. II Timothy 3:16

■ **Does the truth hurt occasionally? Why do people choose not to listen to truth from the Scriptures?**

. . . because the time will come when people will not listen to the true teaching but will find many more teachers who please them by saying the things they want to hear. II Timothy 4:3

■ **Are you welcome to visit the President of the United States and ask him for help? If that door is shut why not try higher authority?**

Let us, then, feel very sure that we can come before God's throne where there is grace. There we can receive mercy and grace to help us when we need it. Hebrews 4:16

■ **How do angels occupy their time?**

All the angels are spirits who serve God and are sent to help those who will receive salvation. Hebrews 1:14

■ **Which person of the Godhead created the world, God the Father, God the Son or God the Holy Spirit?**

God has chosen his Son to own all things, and through him he made the world. Hebrews 1:2

■ **Where is Jesus now and what is He doing?**

Now Jesus has gone into heaven and is at God's right side ruling over angels, authorities, and powers. I Peter 3:22

■ **How can you be sure you know God in a personal way?**

We can be sure that we know God if we obey his commands. I John 2:3

■ **Can you live like Jesus lived?**

Whoever says that he lives in God must live as Jesus lived. I John 2:6

■ **The word gospel means good news. I'll tell you some good news. The gospel says if you make Jesus your Savior you can live forever in heaven. How do you like that good news?**

"For God so loved the world that He gave His only begotten Son, that whoever believes in Him should not perish but have everlasting life." John 3:16 NKJV

■ **I can tell you some bad news too. Everyone is going to live forever, but in Matthew, Chapter 7, it says only a few are going to make it to heaven. If only a few make it to heaven, where will the crowd be going?**

The gate is wide and the road is wide that leads to hell, and many people enter through that gate. Matthew 7:13

■ **If everything in this life and in this world is going to pass away, what should your priorities be?**

The world and everything that people want in it are passing away, but the person who does what God wants lives forever. I John 2:17

■ **Isn't it wonderful that God wants us for His very own kids?**

The Father has loved us so much that we are called children of God. And we really are his children. I John 3:1

■ **Can you commit the same sins continually and say you know Christ?**

So anyone who lives in Christ does not go on sinning. Anyone who goes on sinning has never really understood Christ and has never known him. I John 3:6

■ **Here's a question for all you experts. What is real love?**

This is how we know what real love is: Jesus gave his life for us. I John 3:16

■ **We are fortunate to be alive on God's earth. Did you know that God at one point said He was sorry He had made human beings?**

He was sorry he had made human beings on the earth, and his heart was filled with pain. Genesis 6:6

God created us with the ability to choose between good and evil. Today, like in Genesis 6:6, most people choose not to serve God.

■ **It is estimated there were millions of people on earth at the time of Noah. If it had not been for this one righteous man, God would have destroyed all human beings. We are indeed indebted to Noah. How serious is it to be a righteous person?**

So the LORD said, "I will destroy all human beings that I made on the earth. And I will destroy every animal and everything that crawls on the earth and the birds of the air, because I am sorry I have made them." But Noah pleased the LORD. Genesis 6:7, 8

Everyone who is not righteous will never live with God in heaven— that's how serious it is to be righteous.

■ **Why doesn't the book of Jude list chapters? You have to be an active participant to get the answer. Open your Bible to the book of Jude to solve this mystery.**

The forces of evil are trying to destroy your life each and every day. How often should you open and study your Bible to destroy the activities of the devil? Every day would be a good battle plan to shoot for.

■ **How do you show love toward God?**

Loving God means obeying his commands. I John 5:3

This one is very brief but the meaning speaks volumes.

■ **Are God's commands too difficult to follow?**

And God's commands are not too hard for us . . . . I John 5:3b

■ **You can be a winner; I guarantee it! You can win bigger than any lotto jackpot. The name of the game is Jesus. Want to be a winner?**

So the one who wins against the world is the person who believes that Jesus is the Son of God. I John 5:5

■ **People have written books (Darwin, etc.) and God has authored a Book. Who ya' gonna believe?**

But what God says is more important, and he has told us the truth about his own Son. I John 5:9

■ **How do you get joyful, happy life forever and ever?**

This is what God told us: God has given us eternal life, and this life is in his Son. I John 5:11

You'd think almost everyone would be searching for this life, but in reality only a small number are serious about finding it.

■ **Is it possible a living person does not have life?**

Whoever has the Son [Jesus] has life, but whoever does not have the Son of God does not have life. I John 5:12

I can't express how important spiritual matters are. If you don't choose eternal life through Jesus you are spiritually dead.

■ **If you are a believer, has your eternal life already begun?**

I write this letter to you who believe in the Son of God so you will know you have eternal life.   I John 5:13

Yes, your eternal life begins the moment you accept Jesus Christ as your Savior. Life forever—pass it on.

■ **Who is Christopher Columbus? I do know he had a Norwegian map to follow to America. Who is Leif Ericson? Enough of my Norwegian roots showing through. Here is the real question. Who is eternal life? If you get this right treat yourself to a large pizza.**

And our lives are in the True One and in his Son, Jesus Christ. He is the true God and the eternal life. I John 5:20

■ **Is just "doing wrong" sin?**

Doing wrong is always sin . . . . I John 5:17

■ **Is it true that when the curtain separating the Most Holy Place in the Temple was divinely torn in two, at Jesus' crucifixion, it meant we can now pray directly to God and ask Him for forgiveness of our own sins?**

So, brothers and sisters, we are completely free to enter the Most Holy Place without fear because of the blood of Jesus' death. We can enter through a new and living way that Jesus opened for us. It leads through the curtain—Christ's body. Hebrews 10:19-20

I don't want to leave any doubt. Yes, you can pray and make your confessions directly to God in the authority of Jesus' name.

Chapter Three

"When you have read the Bible, you will know it is the word of God, because you will have found it the key to your own heart, your own happiness, and your own duty."
- Woodrow Wilson -

■ **Do you have to go to church to be a Christian?**

You should not stay away from the church meetings, as some are doing, but you should meet together and encourage each other. Do this even more as you see the day coming. Hebrews 10:25

The answer to the question is no, but advice from God should not be taken lightly. The "day coming" is the day Jesus Christ returns and it is approaching rapidly.

■ **Who replaced animal sacrifice as the final blood sacrifice for sin?**

She will give birth to a son, and you will name him Jesus, because he will save his people from their sins. Matthew 1:21

■ **Is what John the Baptist preached 2000 years ago still pertinent today?**

John said, "Change your hearts and lives because the kingdom of heaven is near." Matthew 3:2

God does not change, people are the same and the message is as pertinent as when John spoke it.

■ **What is the purpose of baptism?**

"I baptize you with water to show that your hearts and lives have changed." Matthew 3:11

■ **What is the Biblical method of baptism? A little water or a lot?**

As soon as Jesus was baptized, he came up out of the water. Matthew 3:16

If you don't agree that immersion is the Biblical way of baptism that's OK; let's not argue over non-essentials. However, we must argue for the essentials of the historic Christian faith. They are: The Bible is without error. Jesus is God and was born of a virgin. Jesus rose from the dead and He is the only way to heaven.

■ **What was the main emphasis of Jesus' preaching?**

From that time Jesus began to preach, saying, "Change your hearts and lives, because the kingdom of heaven is near. Come follow me, and I will make you fish for people." Matthew 4:17, 19

■ **If God calls you into the ministry what should you do?**

So Simon and Andrew immediately left their nets and followed him. Matthew 4:20

■ **Would you like Jesus to talk to you? Do you want to be taught by Jesus? Read His sermon He gave at the Mount of Beatitudes. It is in Matthew, chapters 5, 6, and 7.**

■ **The ugly things people do—where do they come from?**

"It is the thoughtlife that pollutes. For from within, out of men's hearts, come evil thoughts of lust, theft, murder, adultery, wanting what belongs to others, wickedness, deceit, lewdness, envy, slander, pride, and all other folly." Mark 7:20-22 TLB

Many high priced opinions say people are victims of their environment or social conditions. These things do have a bearing on peoples lives but the real root of the problem is between the ears and within the heart.

■ **Are you a fool? Sorry for the pointed question but this is deadly serious stuff.**

"Everyone who hears my words [Jesus'] and does not obey them is like a foolish man who built his house on sand." Matthew 7:26

Fools say to themselves, "There is no God." Psalm 53:1

■ **If you follow Christ with sincerity, will some people mistreat you?**

People will insult you and hurt you. They will lie and say all kinds of evil things about you because you follow me [Christ]. But when they do, you will be happy. Matthew 5:11

If you defend Christ you will experience ridicule. However, there is a good chance you have escaped that because according to Ray Comfort, author, only 3% of Christians tell others about Jesus.

■ **If you suffer because you believe in Jesus, what's in it for you?**

Rejoice and be glad, because you have a great reward waiting for you in heaven. Matthew 5:12

■ **Can adultery be committed without any physical contact?**

But I tell you that if anyone looks at a woman and wants to sin sexually with her, in his mind he has already done that sin with the woman. Matthew 5:28

■ **What should you do to people that hurt you? Usually figure the opposite of what your brain tells you and then your thinking will be more in tune with God's ways.**

"But I say to you, 'Love your enemies. Pray for those who hurt you.' "
Matthew 5:44

■ **The courts allow you to divorce for a number of reasons, but what does God say?**

"The only reason for a man to divorce his wife is if his wife has sexual relations with another man." Matthew 19:9

But if those who are not believers decide to leave, let them leave. When this happens, the Christian man or woman is free. But God called us to live in peace. I Corinthians 7:15

The LORD God of Israel says, "I hate divorce." Malachi 2:16

■ **MUST you forgive others for their wrongdoing against you? What an important question!**

"Yes, if you forgive others for their sins, your Father in heaven will also forgive you for your sins. But if you don't forgive others your Father in heaven will not forgive your sins." Matthew 6:14, 15

When you forgive others for their sins against you it will set you free. It will take away anger. It will give your soul peace.

■ **There is a lot to be said about worrying, but what does Jesus say about it?**

"So I tell you, don't worry about the food or drink you need to live, or about the clothes you need for your body. Life is more than food, and the body is more than clothes. Look at the birds in the air. They don't plant or harvest or store food in barns, but your heavenly Father feeds them. And you know that you are worth much more than the birds. You cannot add any time to your life by worrying about it.

"And why do you worry about clothes? Look at how the lilies in the field grow. They don't work or make clothes for themselves. But I tell you that even Solomon with his riches was not dressed as beautifully as one of these flowers. God clothes the grass in the field, which is alive today but tomorrow is thrown into the fire. So you can be even more sure that God will clothe you. Don't have so little faith! Don't worry and say, 'What will we eat?' or 'What will we drink?' or 'What will we wear?' The people who don't know God keep trying to get these things, and your Father in heaven knows you need them. The thing you should want most is God's kingdom and doing what God wants. Then all these other things you need will be given to you. So don't worry about tomorrow, because tomorrow will have its own worries. Each day has enough trouble of its own." Matthew 6:25-34

■ **What should you desire most out of life?**

"The thing you should want most is God's kingdom and doing what God wants. Then all these other things you need will be given to you." Matthew 6:33

■ **Did the Golden Rule come from the Bible?**

"Do to others what you want them to do to you. This is the meaning of the law of Moses and the teaching of the prophets." Matthew 7:12

■ **How many people do you think are going to heaven? Almost everyone, about half, or just a few?**

"Enter through the narrow gate. The gate is wide and the road is wide that leads to hell, and many people enter through that gate. But the gate is small and the road is narrow that leads to true life [heaven]. Only a **few** [emphasis added] people find that road." Matthew 7:13, 14

■ **How many people do you think are going to hell? Almost everyone, about half, or just a few?**

The answer is in the verse above. This is an important truth and I wanted to emphasize it. Never in my foggiest dreams did I think I would write a book. These words in Matthew, chapter 7, verses 13 and 14 were spoken by Jesus and are the inspiration for my writing. The devil's best work is deception. Most people think they can enter heaven by being good or going to church or some similar reason. Because of those misbeliefs and the two verses above I am doing something my English teachers probably thought was impossible—writing.

■ **You might struggle with believing only a few people make it to heaven but where does absolute truth originate?**

I give you my life. Save me, LORD, God of truth. Psalm 31:5

Jesus answered, "I am the way, and the truth, and the life." John 14:6

"But when the [Holy] Spirit of truth comes, he will lead you into all truth." John 16:13

Truth originates from God the Father, God the Son and God the Holy Spirit.

■ **Have you ever talked to an angel?**

Remember to welcome strangers, because some who have done this have welcomed angels without knowing it. Hebrews 13:2

■ **Are you satisfied with the material possessions you have?**

Keep your lives free from the love of money, and be satisfied with what you have. Hebrews 13:5

■ **God the Father doesn't change, but does Jesus?**

Jesus Christ is the same yesterday, today, and forever. Hebrews 13:8

■ **Is it a sin not to believe Jesus is God?**

He [the Holy Spirit] will prove to them that sin is not believing in me [Jesus]. John 16:9

■ **What is the Holy Spirit's work?**

God planned long ago to choose you by making you his holy people, which is the Spirit's work. I Peter 1:2

■ **Will there ever be a time, as a Christian, when God will leave you?**

God has said, "I will never leave you; I will never forget you." Hebrews 13:5

■ **Can evolution produce love? Hardly!! It can't evolve itself into another species (show me a transitional form) much less create love! Why do we love?**

We love because God first loved us. I John 4:19

■ **I think there is an exact correlation between the six days of creation and the length of history allocated to mankind. I believe each day represents a 1000 year time period. The exciting idea behind this theory is we are only a few years away from the 6000 mark. There were 4000 years from Adam to Jesus and now 2000 years from Jesus' birth to the present. I believe, at the end of 6000 years, Jesus returns for those who believe in Him.**

But do not forget this one thing, dear friends: To the Lord one day is as a thousand years, and a thousand years is as one day. II Peter 3:8

■ **Why did Jesus come to earth?**

"He came to serve others and to give his life as a ransom for many people." Matthew 20:28

■ **I don't want to bring this up but does Jesus address the question of whether we must pay our taxes?**

"So tell us what you think. Is it right to pay taxes to Caesar or not?" Then Jesus said to them, "Give to Caesar the things that are Caesar's, and give to God the things that are God's." Matthew 22:17, 21

■ **What are people going to do in hell forever? Hard question, but the answer is worth knowing.**

"Throw him out into the darkness [hell], where people will cry and grind their teeth with pain." Matthew 22:13

People believe they can go to hell and party with their friends—boy, are they going to be disappointed. If you don't believe people are going to suffer forever I challenge you to prove me wrong. People spend a lot of time studying different topics that will serve them for sixty or seventy years. How much effort do people put into checking out their eternal destiny? Not nearly enough is my researched answer.

■ **Do angels marry?**

"When people rise from the dead, they will not marry, nor will they be given to someone to marry. They will be like the angels in heaven." Matthew 22:30

■ **Most pictures of angels are portrayed as women. But don't all references in the Bible picture angels as men?**

The two angels came to Sodom in the evening as Lot was sitting near the city gate. When he saw them, he got up and went to them and bowed face down on the ground. Lot said, "Sirs. . . ." Genesis 19:1, 2

Yes, references to angels refer to them as all being male.

■ **What did Jesus say were the two most important commands to live by?**

Teacher, which command in the law is the most important? Jesus answered, "Love the Lord your God with all your heart, all your soul, and all your mind. This is the first and most important command. And the second command is like the first: Love your neighbor as you love yourself." Matthew 22:36-39

■ **Which verse made Martin Luther challenge his Catholic beliefs and was the basis for the reformation?**

Now the just shall live by faith . . . . Hebrews 10:38 NKJV

■ **Do you believe that crime, violence and war will diminish? That's good if you do, but why is it things don't seem to be getting any better? The next verses are in red in my Bible—that means they were spoken by Jesus.**

"There will be more and more evil in the world, so most people will stop showing their love for each other. But those people who keep their faith until the end will be saved." Matthew 24:12, 13

A perfect example of this loss of love can be experienced on the local interstate. The road rage of aggressive drivers is almost out of control in city driving. I have literally watched this increase rapidly in the past few years. We can hope violence will diminish, but it is getting "more and more evil" just like Jesus said.

■ **An important factor that proves the Bible is true and inspired by God is the fact that it is the only book of any religion that can tell about events before they happen. Should a book about your future with the words of God in it be at the top of your reading list?**

"Now I [God] have warned you about this before it happens." Matthew 24:25

The LDS Church claims the "Book of Mormon" is God-inspired. True Christians claim only the Bible is inspired. Who is correct? God gives ways of proving that His work is inspired. No proof, no inspiration! The Scriptures tell of events that will happen in the future and then with time these events come to pass (some are described in detail later). They must come to pass correctly each and every time and hundreds and hundreds have already taken place just as predicted. The "Book of Mormon" hasn't had one prediction of a future event occur. Why? The complete work doesn't even attempt trying to predict one future event. No proof, no inspiration! Archaeological evidence is another way to *demonstrate the Bible is inspired. Many <u>ancient</u> towns in Israel mentioned in the Bible are nonexistent today and critics say that is proof of errors in the Scriptures. But one by one through archaeological digs each town is being discovered. The Mormon book speaks of only one <u>modern</u> area called the land of Moroni and they can't prove it ever existed. No proof, no inspiration!*

■ **Many people claim to be Christ, Jesus, the Messiah, or God. An easy way to tell if they are the true Messiah is by the way they announce to the world they have arrived.**

When the Son of Man [Jesus the Christ] comes, he will be seen by everyone, like lightning flashing from the east to the west. At that time, the sign of the Son of Man will appear in the sky. Then all the peoples of the world will cry. They will see the Son of Man coming on clouds in the sky with great power and glory. He will use a loud trumpet to send his angels all around the earth, and they will gather his chosen people from every part of the world. Matthew 24:27, 30, 31

■ **Some don't believe there is an eternal hell. What do you believe?**

"Then the King [God] will say to those on his left, 'Go away from me. You will be punished. Go into the fire that burns forever that was prepared for the devil and his angels. These people will go off to be punished forever, but the good people will go to live forever.' " Matthew 25:41, 46

The answer becomes clearer by comparing these opposites. Light and dark, black and white, love and hate, hot and cold, good and bad, heaven and hell.

■ **Is it a coincidence that Jesus was crucified on the day of Passover? No, because this means He was the sacrificial lamb for our sins. Every detail and every inspired word in the Bible were put there for a purpose.**

After Jesus finished saying all these things, he told his followers, "You know that the day after tomorrow is the day of the Passover Feast. On

that day the Son of Man will be given to his enemies to be crucified."
Matthew 26:1, 2

John said, "Look, the Lamb of God, who takes away the sin of the
world!" John 1:29

■ **Did Jesus know beforehand that He was going to be killed?**

"This woman poured perfume on my body to prepare me for burial."
Matthew 26:12

■ **What body element is necessary for the forgiveness of sin?**

"This blood is poured out for many to forgive their sins." Matthew
26:28

■ **Did any of the apostles who were with Jesus stumble in their
faith?**

Jesus told his followers, "Tonight you will all stumble in your faith on
account of me, because it is written in the Scriptures: 'I will kill the
shepherd, and the sheep will scatter.' " Matthew 26: 31

Don't feel bad if you stumble in your faith, you are only human.

■ **If you are a Christian why do you find yourself doing things you
know you shouldn't do?**

"The spirit wants to do what is right, but the body is weak." Matthew
26:41

■ **Would darkness at high noon be a sign that the person they were
crucifying was who he said he was—the Messiah?**

. . . the robbers who were being crucified beside Jesus also insulted him.
At noon the whole country became dark, and the darkness lasted for
three hours. Matthew 27: 44, 45

It wouldn't get dark in the middle of the day for just anybody—Jesus was God dying for our sins. These events were also chronicled by a reporter of that day. The accounts can be found in the writings of Josephus.

■ **Where did they get the tomb for Jesus' body?**

That evening a rich man named Joseph, a follower of Jesus from the town of Arimathea, came to Jerusalem. Joseph went to Pilate and asked to have Jesus' body. So Pilate gave orders for the soldiers to give it to Joseph ... He put Jesus' body in a new tomb .... Matthew 27:57, 58, 60

When Joseph of Arimathea was contemplating giving his new tomb for Jesus' body, that he had just cut out of solid rock, he said, "Why not? It's only for the weekend!" He didn't actually say that but it does say in Psalms that a merry heart doeth good like a medicine.

■ **Have you heard the story that Jesus' body was stolen while the soldiers guarding it were asleep? They said that's why the tomb was empty on that resurrection morning. I wouldn't believe that if I were you and here's why. That tomb was guarded by topnotch Roman soldiers <u>who knew</u> that if they fell asleep on duty they would be burned alive or crucified. Don't you know those soldiers (at least twelve) were doing all they could to not only stay awake themselves, but to make sure their buddies were staying awake also? The Roman military answer is, "Yes sir!"**

. . . the leading priests and the Pharisees went to Pilate. They said, "Sir, we remember that while that liar was still alive he said, 'After three days I will rise from the dead.' So give the order for the tomb to be guarded closely till the third day. Otherwise, his followers might come and steal the body and tell people that he has risen from the dead. That lie would be even worse than the first one." Pilate said, "Take some soldiers and go guard the tomb the best way you know." So they all went to the tomb and made it safe from thieves by sealing the stone in the entrance and putting soldiers there to guard it. Matthew 27:62-66

■ **Would it surprise you that money and lying were at the root of the story about the Roman soldiers falling asleep on the job?**

Then the priests met with the older Jewish leaders and made a plan. They paid the soldiers a large amount of money and said to them, "Tell the people that Jesus' followers came during the night and stole the body while you were asleep. If the governor hears about this, we will satisfy him and save you from trouble." So the soldiers kept the money and did as they were told. And that story is still spread among the Jewish people even today. Matthew 28:12-15

■ **Do some of your troubles come because God wants to know how true your faith is?**

These troubles come to prove your faith is pure. I Peter 1:7

What book is in most homes? The Bible. What is the best selling book each year? The Bible. What is the least read book in most homes? I suspect it is the Bible and that is too bad because it has all the answers in black and white to any question you have about life.

■ **What is the great commission and are you greatly commissioning?**

Jesus said to his followers, "Go everywhere in the world, and tell the Good News to everyone." Mark 16:15

■ **Can demons actually inhabit humans and if so can they be expelled?**

That evening, after the sun went down, the people brought to Jesus all who were sick and had demons in them. Jesus healed many who had different kinds of sicknesses, and he forced many demons to leave people. Mark 1:32, 34

■ **The thought of a man dying for your sins is interesting, but to know He was God makes all the difference. Jesus was 100 % man** and 100% God at the same time. **Does that sound too hard to believe?**

. . . Jesus Christ. He is the true God and the eternal life. I John 5:20

Your other option is the theory of evolution; is that believable? Its foundation is based on transforming from one species to the next, but not one transitional form has ever been found. The fossil beds would be full of them if evolution were true. This fact alone discredits the theory.

■ **What is one of the main secondary reasons Jesus came to earth?**

Jesus answered, "We should go to other towns around here so I can preach there too." Mark 1:38

■ **Is it a good plan to follow what Jesus did? Have you ever thought, "If I could just get up a little earlier I would have time to read my Bible and pray."**

Early the next morning, while it was still dark, Jesus woke and left the house. He went to a lonely place, where he prayed. Mark 1:35

■ **What is the unforgivable sin?**

"I tell you the truth, all sins that people do and all the things people say against God can be forgiven. But anyone who speaks against the Holy Spirit will never be forgiven; he is guilty of a sin that continues forever." Mark 3:28, 29

Good news! Each and every sin can be forgiven, however, blasphemy against the Holy Spirit cannot be forgiven. Many people get concerned about this sin. The first sign that you have not committed it is that you're concerned. Basically what it means is that you want nothing to do with being saved. So, if you are saved (have accepted Jesus Christ as your Savior), or you want to be saved, you have not committed blasphemy!

■ **Many people hear the teachings of Jesus but they don't stay with them. Is that because His teachings are boring and without life?**

"They hear the teaching and quickly accept it with joy. But since they don't allow the teaching to go deep into their lives, they keep it only a short time. When trouble or persecution comes because of the teaching they accepted, they quickly give up. They hear the teaching, but the worries of this life, the temptation of wealth, and many other evil desires keep the teaching from growing and producing fruit in their lives." Mark 4:16-19

■ **Since Jesus calmed the storm on the sea can't He certainly calm a storm in your life?**

Jesus stood up and commanded the wind and said to the waves, "Quiet! Be still!" Then the winds stopped, and it became completely calm. Mark 4:39

■ **There are different reasons why people go crazy. Is being possessed by an evil spirit one of them?**

When Jesus got out of the boat, instantly a man with an evil spirit came to him from the burial caves. This man lived in the caves, and no one could tie him up, not even with a chain. Many times people had used chains to tie the man's hands and feet, but he always broke them off. No one was strong enough to control him. Day and night he would wander around the burial caves and on the hills, screaming and cutting himself with stones. Mark 5:2

■ **Can more than one evil spirit possess a human being at the same time?**

The demons begged Jesus, "Send us into the pigs; let us go into them." So Jesus allowed them to do this. The evil spirits left the man . . . . Mark 5:12, 13

■ **Did Jesus have brothers and sisters?**

"He is just the carpenter, the son of Mary and the brother of James, Joseph, Judas, and Simon. And his sisters are here with us." Mark 6:3

■ **If your church follows a lot of tradition is it following Jesus or the way of the Pharisees? Is tradition good, bad or unimportant?**

The Pharisees and the teachers of the law said to Jesus, "Why don't your followers obey the unwritten laws which have been handed down to us?" Then Jesus said to them, "You cleverly ignore the commands of God so you can follow your own teachings." Mark 7:5, 9

Tradition is from the human mind. Follow only what comes from God's mind—the Holy Bible.

■ **Are the Pharisees and Sadducees good guys or bad?**

The Pharisees and the Sadducees came to Jesus, wanting to trick him. Matthew 16:1

One way to help remember what the Sadducees stood for is how their name is pronounced, "Sad-you-see."

■ **Is the Bible meant for everyone to understand?**

After Jesus called the crowd to him again, he said, "Every person should listen to me and understand what I am saying." Mark 7:14

Whether God communicates to people in person or by His written Word, the things He says are understandable no matter what your age.

■ **Who is Jesus?**

Peter answered, "You are the Christ." Mark 8:29
Christ means Messiah and Messiah means He is the only one to save you from your sins. The name Jesus means Savior. There is only one door to heaven and that door is Jesus Christ.

I [Jesus] am the door, and the person who enters through me will be saved .... John 10:9

■ **Talking about names, what does the name Satan mean? It means "the enemy." Would you like to choose now between Jesus who wants to be your friend or Satan who wants to be your enemy?**

To accept Jesus as your Savior pray this prayer: "Dear God, I want to live forever in heaven. I want to become a Christian. I confess to you I have sinned and I ask you to forgive me. I believe you sent your only Son Jesus Christ, to die on the Cross to pay for my sins. I believe He rose from the dead and lives today. I place my trust in You and I want to live for You from now on. Thank You for eternal life. Amen."²

■ **With inflation, what is one soul worth in today's dollars?**

"It is worth nothing for them to have the whole world if they lose their souls. They could never pay enough to buy back their souls." Mark 8:36, 37

■ **Is there literal fire in hell and if so does it ever go out?**

"... hell, where the fire never goes out." Mark 9:43

■ **If I told you I am so hungry I could eat a horse, you would know I was just making a point that I was very hungry and had no thought of eating a complete horse. Does the same hold true for the Bible when it uses a figure of speech?**

"If your eye causes you to sin, take it out. It is better for you to enter the kingdom of God with only one eye than to have two eyes and be thrown into hell." Mark 9:47

In other words, if something is causing you to sin, like lust—better to "take it out" of your life rather than hold on to it and end up in hell!

■ So many people, I believe, think God won't forgive them for certain sins they have done. That is wrong. Memorize this and rejoice.

God, you will not reject a heart that is broken and sorry for sin. Psalm 51:17

■ Can God forgive a person for murder? Some might not know, but King David was guilty of murder. This is the verse where he is asking God to forgive him.

God, save me from the guilt of murder, God of my salvation, and I will sing about your goodness. Psalm 51:14

If you are sorry and ask, there is no sin God won't forgive.

■ There are currently some NEW movements within Christianity that are experiential. If it's new do you think it's Biblical?

All things continue the way they have been since the beginning. What has happened will happen again; there is nothing new here on earth. Ecclesiastes 1:9

I like this quotation from radio Bible teacher Greg Laurie. "If it's new it's not true, and if it's true it's not new."

■ Living in this world could warp your brain. Lotteries, Las Vegas, striking it rich, earning big bucks, being envious of people who have a lot of money—that seems to be what's on people's minds. Is that kind of thinking backward to what is good for you?

Then Jesus looked at his followers and said, "How hard it will be for the rich to enter the kingdom of God!" Mark 10:23

Please notice I didn't say having a good job and providing well for your family is wrong. Saving for retirement is a wise and prudent thing to do. The way I read this is rich people tend to put their faith in wealth, and they put God in the back seat and eventually push Him out the door.

■ **Do you have a devastating situation in your life? Read what Jesus said God the Father can do.**

"God can do all things." Mark 10:27

In other words, God can help you. Patience is the key though. The help probably won't be instant like we want. Many times God is using problems to get our attention.

■ **Christian, do you feel you have a lowly position in life or are unimportant compared to others? Well, get all excited. Look what's in your future.**

"Many who have the highest place now will have the lowest place in the future. And many who have the lowest place now will have the highest place in the future." Mark 10:31

■ **Why did Jesus leave heaven to be born into this world?**

"In the same way, the Son of Man did not come to be served. He came to serve others and to give his life as a ransom for many people." Mark 10:45

■ **Can sin be forgiven without blood being shed?**

. . . and sins cannot be forgiven without blood to show death. Hebrews 9:22

Easter is about something besides cute bunnies and Easter eggs!

■ **What is one of the best suggestions from Jesus on how to pray?**

"When you are praying, if you are angry with someone, forgive him so that your Father in heaven will also forgive your sins." Mark 11:25

■ **Add up the true gods from each religion. Plus or minus 10%, how many are there?**

Know and believe today that the LORD is God. He is God in heaven above and on the earth below. There is no other God! Deuteronomy 4:39

■ **The Father is God. Jesus is God. The Holy Spirit is God. How many Gods does that add up to?**

There is <u>one God</u> [emphasis added] and one way human beings can reach God. That way is through Christ Jesus . . . . I Timothy 2:5

"Hear, O Israel: The LORD our God, the <u>LORD is one</u>!" [emphasis added] Deuteronomy 6:4 NKJV

The answer is <u>one God</u> in three persons. The Trinity is probably the most difficult doctrine to comprehend. Hank Hanegraaff, the "Bible Answer Man", puts it this way, "One what, and three who. One essence, three persons."

■ **Can anyone other than God perform miracles?**

"False Christs and false prophets will come and perform great wonders and miracles. They will try to fool even the people God has chosen [Christians], if that is possible. So be careful. I have warned you about all this before it happens." Mark 13:22, 23

■ **One day this earth and the sky above will be totally destroyed, but what one thing will remain?**

"Earth and sky will be destroyed, but the words I [Jesus] have said will never be destroyed." Mark 13:31

■ **What had Jesus done to be worthy of crucifixion?**

The leading priests and the whole Jewish council tried to find something that Jesus had done wrong so they could kill him. But the council could find no proof of anything. Mark 14:55

■ At nine o'clock in the morning most people are thinking about what they will have for coffee break. Was that also the exact time Jesus was nailed on the Cross to pay the ultimate sacrifice for our sins?

It was nine o'clock in the morning when they crucified Jesus. There was a sign with this charge against Jesus written on it: THE KING OF THE JEWS. Mark 15:25, 26

■ How many hours did Jesus hang on the Cross before He died?

It was about noon, and the whole land became dark until three o'clock in the afternoon, because the sun did not shine. The curtain in the Temple was torn in two. Jesus cried out in a loud voice, "Father, I give you my life." After Jesus said this, he died. Luke 23:44-46

Numbers are significant in the Bible. The number for mankind is six. Jesus spent six hours on the Cross signifying He did it all for mankind. Thank you, Jesus.

■ Will the fires of hell ever be put out?

"He will put the good part of the grain into his barn, but he will burn the chaff with a fire that cannot be put out." Luke 3:17

The parts of the grain are referring to good and bad people.

■ You can blame the devil for urging you on, but don't most evil thoughts originate in your own mind?

"Out of the mind come evil thoughts, murder, adultery, sexual sins, stealing, lying, and speaking evil of others." Matthew 15:19

■ Where did the Christian symbol of the dove come from?

While Jesus was praying, heaven opened and the Holy Spirit came down on him in the form of a dove. Then a voice came from heaven saying,

"You are my Son, whom I love, and I am very pleased with you." Luke 3:21, 22

Some of these questions are similar to others, but if you are like me it takes reading something a few times to really make it stick. By reading this book you could become your own Bible answer person.

■ **What happened at high noon the day they crucified Jesus that should have clued people in that Jesus was who He said He was?**

It was about noon, and the whole land became dark until about three o'clock in the afternoon, because the sun did not shine. The curtain in the Temple was torn in two. Luke 23:44, 45

Chapter Four

"That Book, sir, is the rock on which our republic rests."
- *Andrew Jackson* -

■ **Why do the gospels (Matthew, Mark, Luke and John) all sound alike?**

After the Lord Jesus said these things to his followers, he was carried up into heaven, and he sat at the right side of God. Mark 16:19

While he was blessing them, he was separated from them and carried into heaven. Luke 24:51

It's because the gospels are an account of some of the same things as written by four different people.

■ **Sometimes it's simple insights that have the greatest impact. Back in the mid 70's I watched the TV mini-series *Roots* and that sparked my interest to research our family tree. No one had written the family history down on the paternal side and I soon found out how difficult it was to trace back further than people could remember. After 15 years of digging I made it back only five generations. Then one day I was reading in Luke where it lists the family history of Jesus. It is almost a whole page of so-and-so was the son of so-and-so and so-and-so was the son of so-and-so, etc. I almost skipped that page, but I read each of those generations—77 in all. When I got done I knew that had to be inspired. With my experience I knew no one could dig up this much family history— even if half of it had been written down. Plus it wasn't even Luke's family tree so the interest wouldn't be there to drive him on. Don't** you think discovering these little proofs of authenticity yourself would make reading the Bible very interesting?

When Jesus began his ministry, he was about thirty years old. People thought that Jesus was Joseph's son. Joseph was the son of Heli. Heli was the son of Matthat. Matthat was the son of Levi. Levi was the son of Melki, etc. Luke 3:23, 24

■ **Do you believe there are guardian angels watching over you?**

He has put his angels in charge of you to watch over you wherever you go. Psalm 91:11

■ **Why did I decide to write this book? This next verse partly explains why.**

Then Jesus said to those Jews who believed Him, "If you abide in My word, you are My disciples indeed. And you shall know the truth, and the truth shall make you free." John 8:31, 32 NKJV

Please notice in the preceding verse Jesus did not say a particular church, minister or priest has to interpret the Scriptures for you. This truth alone can set you free. God had the Scriptures written for YOU! Going to a good church is a wonderful thing, but making it to heaven is your responsibility. That means you personally have to know what's in the Bible to be able to test your pastor or church to know that what they are telling you is valid. Your salvation and your eternal life depend on what you believe. This is more important than anything—find out for yourself what God's word says.

The Bereans were eager to hear what Paul and Silas [teachers of Scripture] said and studied the Scriptures every day to find out if these things were true. Acts 17:11

■ **Will doing good works help get you into heaven?**

I mean that you have been saved by grace through believing. You did not save yourselves; it was a gift from God. It was not the result of your own efforts, so you cannot brag about it. Ephesians 2:8, 9

If you thought the answer was yes then you need to read for yourself what God's word says. You simply can't work your way to heaven. Paying money to your church will not help you get to heaven either. Salvation is a totally free gift. Once your salvation is assured you will want to do good works and give money to God's work, but those things by themselves have no bearing on your entering heaven.

■ **What Scripture reference is it they always hold up at football games?**

"God loved the world so much that he gave his one and only Son so that whoever believes in him may not be lost, but have eternal life." John 3:16

■ **Don't feel bad if you are rejected when telling others about the gospel. Wasn't even Jesus kicked out of His own home town after preaching to them?**

When all the people in the synagogue heard these things, they became very angry. They got up, forced Jesus out of town [Nazareth], and took him to the edge of the cliff on which the town was built. They planned to throw him off the edge, but Jesus walked through the crowd and went on his way. Luke 4:28-30

■ **Why did the Jewish teachers of the law and the Pharisees hate Jesus so much?**
        a. Because He claimed He was God?
        b. Because He claimed He was God?
        c. Because He claimed He was God?
        d. All the above?

Seeing their faith, Jesus said, "Friend, your sins are forgiven." The Jewish teachers of the law and the Pharisees thought to themselves,

"Who is this man who is speaking as if he were God? Only God can forgive sins." Luke 5:20, 21

■ **Who is Lord of the Sabbath day?**

Then Jesus said to the Pharisees, "The Son of Man [Jesus] is Lord of the Sabbath day." Luke 6:5

■ **Would you think better thoughts if someone always knew what you were thinking?**

But he [Jesus] knew what they were thinking . . . . Luke 6:8

■ **How much time should you devote to prayer over a major decision?**

At that time Jesus went off to a mountain to pray, and he spent the night praying to God. The next morning, Jesus called his followers to him and chose twelve of them, whom he named apostles . . . . Luke 6:12, 13

■ **Could your quality of life make a dramatic improvement if you followed these principles?**

"But I say to you who are listening, love your enemies. Do good to those who hate you, bless those who curse you, pray for those who are cruel to you." Luke 6:27, 28

The answer is yes, but you won't find out until you try it.

■ **How can God's wisdom help you in daily life? I had a neighbor who knowingly kept something I loaned him. That situation really bothered me until I discovered the principal of loving your enemy. That is not easy; but it works.**

Love your enemies . . . implore God's blessing on those who hurt you . . . when things are taken away from you, don't worry about getting them back. Treat others as you want them to treat you. Luke 6:27-31 TLB

■ One way God communicates with us is through His Holy Bible. Could He speak to us audibly if the rare occasion were to arise?

A voice [God the Father] came from the cloud, saying, "This is my Son, whom I have chosen. Listen to him!" Luke 9:35

■ I wanted to be a farmer and now I realize I have been doing that type of work in a spiritual way. Can people be harvested into the Kingdom of God?

"There are a great many people to harvest, but there are only a few workers. So pray to God, who owns the harvest, that he will send more workers to help gather his harvest." Luke 10:2

■ How many of your friends or people you know talk to you about Jesus or the Bible? I would venture to say none or very few. Why is that?

"There are a great many people to harvest, but there are only a few workers." Luke 10:2a

■ What's the very best thing to be happy about?

"But you should not be happy because the spirits obey you but because your names are written in heaven." Luke 10:20

People are very particular about their name and rightfully so. If it gets misspelled, mispronounced, used in a derogatory way or someone doesn't remember it, that's a touchy area. Whose name is looked up in a new phone book to make sure it's there? If important reservations have been made it could get explosive if they can't find your name. In heaven there is the Book of Life in which your name must be written in order for you to enter God's Kingdom. How many people bother to check to make sure their name is written in the most important place—heaven?

■ How does your name become written in heaven?

If you use your mouth to say, "Jesus is Lord," and if you believe in your heart that God raised Jesus from the dead, you will be saved. We believe with our hearts, and so we are made right with God. And we use our mouths to say that we believe, and so we are saved. Romans 10:9, 10

■ **Which church is the "true church?"**

. . .[people] whose names are written in the book of life. Philippians 4:3

The "true church" is composed of people whose names are written in heaven! No matter what church or denomination you belong to if your name is not written in heaven (by being born again) you don't belong to the "true church."

■ **Is measuring your life by what you own a good standard?**

Then Jesus said to them, "Be careful and guard against all kinds of greed. Life is not measured by how much one owns." Luke 12:15

■ **And what eventually happens to all those things you own?**

Then I can say to myself, "I have enough good things stored to last for many years. Rest, eat, drink, and enjoy life!" But God said to him, 'Foolish man! Tonight your life will be taken from you. So who will get those things you have prepared for yourself?' This is how it will be for those who store up things for themselves and are not rich toward God." Luke 12:19, 20, 21

This can probably be summed up best by a saying my dad sent me. "The moment you die, everything you had now belongs to someone else."

■ **Figuring out life is a job in itself. Throw in the spiritual aspect and it gets very interesting. With that said, do evil spirits cause some people to be crippled?**

A woman was there who, for eighteen years, had an evil spirit in her that made her crippled. Luke 13:11

■ I would venture to say almost everyone would like to go to heaven, wouldn't you agree? But the shocking truth is only a few live by the Bible and will make it.

Someone said to Jesus, "Lord, will only a few people be saved?" Jesus said, "Try hard to enter through the narrow door, because many people will try to enter there, but they will not be able." Luke 13:23, 24

They won't be able to enter because of themselves, not because of God. The way to heaven is repentance and forgiveness of sins through Jesus Christ.

■ What is the important answer as to why more people aren't going to heaven?

"And this is the condemnation, that the light [Jesus and His teachings] has come into the world, and men loved darkness rather than light, because their deeds were evil. John 3:1 NKJV

You might have just said, "My deeds are not evil!" You can think that, but if you have not accepted Jesus as your Savior the Scriptures say you are against Him.

■ What is one way to know the Bible is true?

So Judas threw the money into the Temple. So what Jeremiah the prophet had said came true: "They took thirty silver coins. That is how little the Israelites thought he was worth." Matthew 27:5, 9

The Bible describes events in detail before they happen. Only God's inspired Word can predict 100% accurately what will happen in the future. The words from Jeremiah were written down in 640-586 B.C. and the actual event followed in A.D. 32.

■ Who do you think is going to have a high place of honor in heaven? Could it be a prominent pastor, an evangelist or a grandmother who prayed for her grandchildren to follow Jesus? We don't know for sure, but this Scripture gives us some insight.

"There are those who have the lowest place in life now who will have the highest place in the future. And there are those who have the highest place now who will have the lowest place in the future." Luke 13:30

■ **Would you like to be great now and then be made humble, or be humble now and then be made great?**

"All who make themselves great will be made humble, but those who make themselves humble will be made great." Luke 14:11

■ **Who can you have over for dinner where you get the blessing?**

Then Jesus said to the man who had invited him, "When you give a lunch or a dinner, don't invite only your friends, your family, your other relatives, and your rich neighbors. At another time they will invite you to eat with them, and you will be repaid. Instead when you give a feast, invite the poor, the crippled, the lame, and the blind. Then you will be blessed, because they have nothing and cannot pay you back. But you will be repaid when the good people rise from the dead." Luke 14:12-14

By now you should be seeing that the way we think is not the way God thinks.

■ **In order to be a follower of Jesus whom must you love more than anyone?**

Large crowds were traveling with Jesus, and he turned and said to them, "If anyone comes to me but loves his father, mother, wife, children, brothers, or sisters—or even life—more than me, he cannot be my follower." Luke 14:25, 26

You probably answered this question correctly but do you practice it? Why do I have to get so personal? Because I know the Bible says only a few really love Jesus. Yes, I am getting on your case. Why? Because so many would love to get to heaven, but they love the things of this life more than Jesus!

■ There is—read my lips—no pain in heaven. How about in the "other place?"

"In the place of the dead [hell] he was in much pain." Luke 16:23

■ At what point in time did they stop preaching the laws of Moses?

"The law of Moses and the writings of the prophets were preached until John [the Baptist] came." Luke 16:16

John the Baptist was born approximately the same time as Jesus.

■ Can you have worldly riches and serve God? Sure. Can you serve worldly riches and serve God at the same time?

"No servant can serve two masters. The servant will hate one master and love the other, or will follow one master and refuse to follow the other. You cannot serve both God and worldly riches." Luke 16:13

■ Are you really dead after you die?

Later, Lazarus died, and the angels carried him to the arms of Abraham. The rich man died, too, and was buried . . . . The rich man saw Abraham far away with Lazarus at his side. Luke 16:22, 23

The real you, your soul, lives on forever no matter if in hell or heaven.

■ Do you think it's going to be "cool" to go to hell and party with your friends?

"He called, 'Father Abraham, have mercy on me! Send Lazarus to dip his finger in water and cool my tongue, because I am suffering in this fire.' " Luke 16:24

■ If you make the biggest mistake of your life and find yourself in hell after death, how in heaven's name would you get out of there?

". . . and no one can leave there [hell] and come here [paradise]." Luke 16:26

Uh, oh, BIG MISTAKE!

■ **If someone came to you and offered for free a fabulous estate in some exotic place and a guarantee to pay all your future bills, wouldn't that be cause for excitement?**

"Don't fear, little flock, because your Father wants to give you the kingdom." Luke 12:32

■ **Would most people listen if someone they knew came back from the dead and told them heaven and hell really exist?**

"The rich man said, 'No father Abraham! If someone goes to them from the dead, they would believe and change their hearts and lives.' " But Abraham said to him, 'If they will not listen to Moses and the prophets, they will not listen to someone who comes back from the dead.' " Luke 16:30, 31

For our time, instead of "Moses and the prophets," you could substitute modern preachers and things of the Bible.

■ **It's one thing for you to sin, but whom must you not cause to sin?**

It would be better for you to be thrown into the sea with a large stone around your neck than to cause one of these little ones [children] to sin. So be careful! Luke 17:2, 3

■ **Will there be a disabling monetary crash in the United States prior to Jesus' coming again at the Rapture?**

When the Son of Man comes again . . . . It will be the same as during the time of Lot. People were eating, drinking, buying, selling, planting, and building. Luke 17:26, 28

I don't believe all the rhetoric these prophets of doom are spouting concerning an imminent financial collapse because of the above and related Scriptures. I believe we are near the period of time, "when the Son of Man comes again." You can't have a financial collapse and have life operating normally like you just read. I put my money on the "profits" of boom. However, during the Tribulation period, that follows the Rapture, there will be financial collapse and inflation like never before.

■ **Will gold and silver be of any value in a financial meltdown during the end time seven year Tribulation period?**

The people will throw their silver into the streets, and their gold will be like trash. Their silver and gold will not save them from the LORD'S anger. Ezekiel 7:19

Precious metals are a good hedge against inflation and will be very valuable for a time during that period. People throwing their gold and silver into the streets toward the end of the Tribulation give quite an insight into how terrible that time will be.

■ **Do you have to be a scholar, an intellect, or even smart to figure out how to enter the kingdom of God?**

"I tell you the truth, you must accept the kingdom of God as if you were a child, or you will never enter it." Luke 18:17

John Zachary, author, sums this up well, "Salvation is simple, but churches make it difficult. We trip over the simple concept of salvation by faith."

■ **What is the purpose of the Son of Man (Jesus) coming to earth?**

"The Son of Man came to find lost people and save them." Luke 19:10

■ **Is it possible for an angel to die?**

"In that life they are like angels and cannot die." Luke 20:36

■ **Are there degrees of punishment in hell?**

"But they cheat widows and steal their houses and then try to make themselves look good by saying long prayers. They will receive a greater punishment [in hell]." Luke 20:47

■ **What are several main reasons for the seven years of Tribulation in the end times?**

For when Your judgments are in the earth, the inhabitants of the world will learn righteousness. Isaiah 26:9 NKJV

"These are the days of punishment to bring about all that is written in the Scriptures." Luke 21:22

Good news! Anyone who has trusted in Jesus prior to this time of trouble will not be a part of this punishment.

However, let's say you used poor judgment and have not trusted Jesus for salvation and now find yourself in the Tribulation period; what do you do now? All true living believers have been removed from earth to heaven. Therefore any "Christian" church that still has most, if not all, of its pastoral staff still in place is the first place you want to avoid. Obviously they were not teaching that Jesus is the only way to heaven. Deception will be lord during this time. Believable false stories will be flying as to why all the Christians disappeared. The only true story of this event is in the New Testament. Read and study the New Testament starting with the book of John—your eternal life now depends on it. Ask Jesus for forgiveness of your sins. Believe in Him and ask Him to save your soul. Hang on to your new faith at ALL cost and prepare to die for it. Even at the threat of death do not take "the mark" in your forehead or right hand that your government will try forcing on you. More than likely you will need this mark to survive. But if you take it your soul will be condemned because by taking the mark you will agree to worship Antichrist as God instead of Jesus Christ. Weigh heavily a short time of suffering for an eternity full of joy and happiness.

■ The seven year Tribulation period will affect the whole world. But what people and land is the focus of it? I will give you a hint. Why is the little country of Israel in the news so much?

"Great trouble will come upon this land [Israel], and God will be angry with these people." Luke 21:23

■ People assume things are going to continue on about the same or even get better. Sorry to burst that bubble, but we now have weapons that can blow up every nation on earth, and not just once but many times over. Let me ask you, "Have there been major weapon systems built that were not used?" It's only a matter of time. There was World War I, World War II and it is likely Armageddon (final world war before Jesus returns to earth) may soon be at hand?

"On earth, nations will be afraid and confused because of the roar and fury of the sea [sea here refers to people]. People will be so afraid they will faint, wondering what is happening to the world, because the powers of the heavens will be shaken. Then people will see the Son of Man coming in a cloud with power and great glory. When these things begin to happen, look up and hold your heads high, because the time when God will free you is near!" Luke 21:25-28

Am I a doom and gloomer? I am just reporting Bible prophecy and prophecy is news before it happens. Thank goodness true Christians are going to be absent during the battle of Armageddon. What is a true Christian? I'm sure glad you asked that. A true Christian is one who has a personal relationship with the God of this universe—Jesus Christ.

■ The earth is not totally destroyed during Armageddon, but will it be someday?

Earth and sky will be destroyed . . . . Luke 21:33

One reason I am trying to train myself not to get "all shook up" (Can you tell I was a teenager when Elvis was king of rock 'n roll?) about earthly fame and wealth or go overboard on "things" is because one day the earth itself will be burned up and destroyed. Call 1-800-END OF THE WORLD to find out the date. If you don't appreciate my telephone number humor call 1-800-NOT FUNNY MIKE.

■ **What one thing will not be destroyed when the whole world is destroyed?**

". . . but the words I [Jesus] have spoken will never be destroyed." Luke 21:33b

When the world is destroyed 1000 years after the Tribulation, Jesus creates a new one. This will then be home for eternity to everyone who has put their faith in God.

■ **Do you want to know within a generation when Jesus is coming back to rule the world? You would have to know a key point in this next Scripture in order for it to make sense. Check it out. You will find the fig tree represents Israel.**

"And Jerusalem will be trampled by Gentiles until the times of the Gentiles are fulfilled." [This prophecy was fulfilled when Israel re-took control of Jerusalem in the six day war on June 7, 1967.] And He spoke to them a parable: "Look at the fig tree, and all the trees. When they are already budding, you see and know for yourselves that summer is now near. So you, likewise, when you see these things happening, know that the kingdom of God is near. Assuredly, I say to you, this generation [emphasis added] will by no means pass away till all things are fulfilled." Luke 21:24, 29-32 NKJV

■ **What "got into" Judas Iscariot to make him want to betray the Lord?**

Satan entered Judas Iscariot, one of Jesus' twelve apostles. Luke 22:3

Satan does not just come into you—it's your choice to let him in.

■ **What happens to you once the devil has used you for his deeds?**

So Judas threw the money into the Temple.   Then he went off and hanged himself. Matthew 27:5

■ **Who did Jesus spill His blood for?**

In the same way, after supper, Jesus took the cup and said, "This cup is the new agreement that God makes with his people.   This new agreement begins with my blood which is poured out for you." Luke 22:20

■ **The next time you are in a restaurant, try answering this question from Jesus' way of thinking. "Who is more important— the customer or the waiter/waitress?"**

"Who is more important: the one sitting at the table or the one serving? You think the one at the table is more important, but I [Jesus] am like a servant among you." Luke 22:27

As Christians we need to learn to serve others.

■ **Will there be eating and drinking in heaven?**

". . . so you may eat and drink at my [God's] table in my kingdom." Luke 22:30

■ **If a person were born in Bethlehem, yet existed before creation, would he qualify to be God?**

O Bethlehem Ephrathah, you are but a small Judean village, yet you will be the birthplace of my King who is alive from everlasting ages past! Micah 5:2 TLB

■ **Because God knows best, what phrase should we use in our prayers that Jesus used?**

"Father, . . . do what you want, not what I want." Luke 22:42

■ Faith teachers proclaim if you have enough faith you will receive healing, financial blessings, etc. But if you don't get what you pray for, whose fault is it? Why, of course, it's yours because you didn't muster up the proper amount of faith. Thank goodness my Bible doesn't put the blame on me.

And so God's blessings are not given just because someone decides to have them or works hard to get them. They are given because God takes pity on those he wants to. Romans 9:16 TLB

■ If you do some deep pondering about life, shouldn't you come to the conclusion that it doesn't make sense to struggle through life and then be rewarded with death that ends it all?

"Why are you looking for a living person in this place for the dead? He [Jesus] is not here; he has risen from he dead." Luke 24:5, 6

Thank goodness the Bible has a good ending for us. Jesus rose from the dead and so will people who believe in Him.

■ The preaching of the gospel started in what city?

" . . . and that a change of hearts and lives and forgiveness of sins would be preached in his name to all nations, starting at Jerusalem." Luke 24:47

Chapter Five

■ **What sets Christianity apart from all other religions? It's that our Savior, Jesus Christ, is God! Is, in fact, Jesus Christ, God?**

In the beginning there was the Word. The Word was with God, and the Word was God. John 1:1

The Word became a human and lived among us. We saw his glory—the glory that belongs to the only Son of the Father—and he was full of grace and truth. John 1:14

He [Jesus] is dressed in a robe, dipped in blood, and his name is the Word of God. Revelation 19:13

"The Father and I [Jesus] are one." John 10:30

We should live like that while we wait for our great hope and the coming of the glory of our great God and Savior Jesus Christ. Titus 2:13

We also know that the Son of God has come and has given us understanding so that we can know the True One. And our lives are in the True One and in his Son, Jesus Christ. He [Jesus] is the true God and the eternal life. I John 5:20

But he [Jesus] did not think that being equal with God was something to be used for his own benefit. But he gave up his place with God and made himself nothing. He was born to be a man and became like a servant. Philippians 2:6, 7

Were you born to die? No. Was Jesus born to die? Yes.

How can Jesus be equal with God if He is the Son of God? Because Jesus didn't become the Son of God until temporarily limiting Himself when He came to be born of a virgin.

■ **Are there any flaws in the Word of God?**

The teachings of the LORD are perfect; they give new strength. Psalm 19:7

If you haven't read the Bible seriously before, should you start reading it from the front? Most often it is recommended that you start with the book of John. Then read the rest of the flawless New Testament from the beginning.

■ **I believe the Trinity is in the first three verses of Genesis. What do you think? Look for God in verse 1, the Holy Spirit in verse 2 and Jesus in verse 3. Verses 1 & 2 are easy, but here is a hint for verse 3. It begins with, "Then God said." The words of John 1:1 and 1:14 relate the word "said" to Jesus. "In the beginning there was the word ["Then God said."] and "The word became a human [Jesus]and lived among us."**

(1) In the beginning God created the sky and the earth. (2) The earth was empty and had no form. Darkness covered the ocean, and God's Spirit was moving over the water. (3) Then God said, "Let there be light," and there was light. Genesis 1:1-3

■ **Did God the Father or Jesus actually create the world?**

In the beginning there was the Word. The Word was with God and the Word was God. He was with God in the beginning. All things were made by him, and nothing was made without him [Jesus]. John 1:1-3

Sal Giardina, scientist, suggests God the Father was the architect, Jesus was the creator and the Holy Spirit provided the energy.

■ **Did Jesus' own people, the Jews, reject Him?**

He came to the world that was his own, but his own people did not accept him. But to all who did accept him and believe in him he gave the right to become children of God. John 1:11, 12

■ **Jesus was born after John the Baptist but lived before him. Isn't only God eternal?**

John tells the truth about him and cries out, saying, "This is the One I told you about: 'The One who comes after me is greater than I am, because he [Jesus] was living before me.' " John 1:15

■ **Where did grace and truth come from? Wasn't it Oceanside, CA?**

The law was given through Moses, but grace and truth came through Jesus Christ. John 1:17

■ **Has anyone ever seen God the Father?**

No one has ever seen God. John 1:18a

■ **If no one has ever seen God the Father, how do we know what he is like?**

No one has ever seen God. But God the only Son is very close to the Father, and he has shown us what God is like. John 1:18

■ **Why is Jesus called the Lamb of God?**

The next day John saw Jesus coming toward him. John said, "Look, the Lamb of God, who takes away the sin of the world!" John 1:29

In the Old Testament people offered lambs as a sacrifice for their sins and in the New Testament Jesus offered himself as the final sacrifice for our sins.

■ **Was Jesus psychic?**

He did not need anyone to tell him about people, because he knew what was in people's minds. John 2:25

No, He wasn't psychic. He was the God man. That means he was 100 % God and 100% man at the same time. That's how He knew what people were thinking.

■ **Jimmy Carter popularized the term "born again." Is that phrase found in the Scriptures?**

Jesus answered, "I tell you the truth, unless one is born again he cannot be in God's kingdom." John 3:3

■ **Do you have to be "born again" to enter heaven?**

Jesus answered, "I tell you the truth, unless one is born again he cannot be in God's kingdom." John 3:3

■ **What is a good explanation of being born again?**

Nicodemus said, "But if a person is already old, how can he be born again? He cannot enter his mother's body again. So how can a person be born a second time?" But Jesus answered, "I tell you the truth, unless one is born from water [mother's womb] and the Spirit [spiritual birth], he cannot enter God's kingdom." John 3:4, 5

■ **What happens spiritually when we are born again?**

"Human life comes from human parents, but spiritual life comes from the Spirit. Don't be surprised when I [Jesus] tell you, 'You must all be born again.' " John 3:6, 7

But God's mercy is great, and he loved us very much. Though we were spiritually dead because of the things we did against God, he gave us new life with Christ. Ephesians 2:4, 5

We are triune just like God who is Father, Son and Holy Spirit. We are made up of body, soul and spirit. The spirit in all of humankind died when Adam and Eve sinned, and so it is the spirit that needs to be reborn from above.

■ **Does Adam and Eve's sin affect us today?**

One man [Adam] sinned, and so death ruled all people because of that one man. Romans 5:17

Some spiritual matters can be difficult to apprehend. The reason we have to be born again stems all the way back to when the human spirit died when Adam and Eve sinned.

■ **Can you imagine standing in front of a judge hearing him pronounce a sentence of life in prison? Imagine standing in front of God hearing him pronounce, "You did not believe in my Son. Away with you to the lake of fire for eternity!"**

People who believe in God's Son are not judged guilty. John 3:18

Don't get nervous about this because salvation is simple. The problem comes from rejecting Jesus Christ as your Savior. Some of the strongest believers are people who set out to disprove the Bible and the accounts in it. They found the evidence totally proves the Scriptures as being accurate and true instead of inaccurate and false. One such person was Josh McDowell. I suggest his books: <u>Evidence That Demands a Verdict</u>, and <u>More Than a Carpenter</u>.

■ **What important task does God tell you to work at?**

Jesus answered, "The work God wants you to do is this: Believe the One he sent." John 6:29

■ **Can you be holy or is that only an attribute for God, Jesus and the Holy Spirit?**

It is written in the Scriptures: "You [believers] must be holy, because I [God] am holy." I Peter 1:16

■ **Did Jesus own a house? No He didn't, nor did He own a Corvette (donkey). Where did Jesus stay if He didn't own a house?**

But Jesus replied, "Remember, I don't even own a place to lay my head. Foxes have dens to live in, and birds have nests, but I, the Messiah, have no earthly home at all." Luke 9:58 TLB

After this, Jesus and his followers went into the area of Judea, where he stayed with his followers . . . . John 3:22

■ **What specific food does God tell you to work for?**

Jesus answered, "I tell you the truth, you aren't looking for me because you saw me do miracles. You are looking for me because you ate the bread and were satisfied. Don't work for the food that spoils. Work for the food [Bread of Life] that stays good always and gives eternal life. The Son of Man will give you this food . . . . John 6:26, 27

■ **Who is the Bread of Life? No, it's not Mr. Wonder Bread.**

"God's bread is the One who comes down from heaven and gives life to the world." Then Jesus said, "I am the bread that gives life. Whoever comes to me will never be hungry [spiritually] . . . ." John 6:33, 35

■ **What did God serve in the desert restaurant for forty years and what type of food was it like?**

"Our fathers ate the manna in the desert. This is written in the Scriptures: 'He gave them bread from heaven to eat.' " John 6:31

■ **You have a choice to accept Jesus, but does Jesus have a choice to accept you?**

The Father gives me my people. Every one of them will come to me, and I will always accept them. John 6:37

■ **Was Jesus successful in witnessing to all of His own family?**

(Even Jesus' brothers did not believe in him.) John 7:5

Let your light shine bright and don't be discouraged if you have a difficult time sharing your faith with family.

■ **What is the root cause of why people hate Christianity?**

Jesus said to his brothers, ". . . the world cannot hate you, but it hates me, because I tell it the evil things it does." John 7:6, 7

■ **Does darkness overcome light or does light overcome darkness?**

In him there was life, and that life was the light of all people. The Light shines in the darkness, and the darkness has not overpowered it. John 1:4, 5

■ **We saw where Jesus was the bread of life, but who is the light of the world?**

Later, Jesus talked to the people again, saying, "I am the light of the world. The person who follows me will never live in darkness but will have the light that gives life." John 8:12

■ **If God is not your Father, then who is?**

You belong to your father the devil . . . . John 8:44a

When dealing with spiritual matters your choices are limited to two. And uncertainty is not one of the choices.

■ **He was a murderer from the beginning and is the father of lies. Who is this fallen angel?**

. . . the devil . . . . He was a murderer from the beginning and was against the truth, because there is no truth in him. When he tells a lie, he shows what he is really like, because he is a liar and the father of lies. John 8:44

■ **Will people, even your family, sometimes sharply criticize your Christian beliefs?**

Jesus answered . . . . "Why are you trying to kill me?" The people answered, "A demon has come into you." John 7:16, 19, 20

You will be criticized, but stay strong in your beliefs. People even said to Jesus' face that He had a demon in Him, but that would have been impossible.

■ Did you know that in the Old Testament, under the law, they used to kill people for adultery?

They said to Jesus, "This woman was caught having sexual relations with a man who is not her husband. The law of Moses commands that we stone to death every woman who does this. What do you say that we should do?" John 8:4, 5

The sin of adultery is still the same, but instead of being stoned immediately, because we are under God's grace, He now gives us our whole life to get our act together. Thank you Jesus.

■ Are there do-it-yourself tests to see if you belong to God?

"The person who belongs to God accepts what God says." John 8:47

Yes, there are many of these tests.

■ How did Jesus protect Himself from the devil?

Jesus said to the devil, "Go away from me, Satan! It is written in the Scriptures . . . ." Matthew 4:10

The way you can protect yourself from evil is to know "what is written." Start with the book of John; your life will never be the same.

■ Does God exist in time as we know it?

Jesus answered, "I tell you the truth, before Abraham was even born, I am!" John 8:58

With the pronouncement of "I am" Jesus was saying He is eternal—past, present and future. Since Jesus has lived eternally in the past what does it mean in Genesis 1:1 when it says, "In the beginning God . . . "? That was the beginning of time for people and God exists outside of what we know as time. That's how God can tell us what is going to happen in the future.

■ **I know people who say they are Christian, but they use the Lord's name carelessly and even in vain. Are they really Christians? We can't judge people's hearts, but I know I don't want God calling me His enemy!**

God . . . . They say evil things about you. Your enemies use your name thoughtlessly. Psalm 139:19, 20

■ **These same people I mentioned in the previous item probably don't read their Bible much, if at all. I know that is a hard statement, but if God is calling you His enemy it's time for a reality check, isn't it? If they read their Bible they would come across Scriptures like the following:**

God, examine me and know my heart; test me and know my nervous thoughts. See if there is any bad thing in me. Lead me on the road to everlasting life. Psalm 139:23, 24

■ **Do you have trouble understanding and comprehending how great and wonderful God is? Don't let that bother you; you're not alone.**

The LORD is great and worthy of our praise; no one can understand how great he is. Psalm 145:3

■ **Did the virgin Mary have a choice about giving birth to the Son of God?**

Mary said, "I am the servant of the Lord. Let this happen to me as you say!" Then the angel went away. Luke 1:38

Yes, Mary had a choice. Was she the mother of God? God has always existed and had no parents, but Mary was the mother of Jesus. Jesus was fully a man but also God at the same time (the incarnate God). Mary was the mother of Jesus' manhood—she did not give birth to God.

■ **Is Mary deity?**

Then Mary said, "My soul praises the Lord; my heart rejoices in God my Savior, because he has shown his concern for his humble servant girl." Luke 1:46-48

If Mary is deity she would be God and wouldn't need a Savior. In this Scripture Mary calls God her Savior.

■ **Is there anywhere in the Bible it says to pray to someone other than God?**

"When you pray ... pray to your Father who cannot be seen." Matthew 6:6

Jesus said to them, "When you pray, say: 'Father ....' " Luke 11:2

The answer is no, so it would be improper to address prayers to Abraham, the Father of the Jews, Mary or Saint Bernard. These subjects can get real serious, especially if I am stepping on some feet, so if you are wondering who Saint Bernard is, think in terms of four feet.

■ **I always thought from hearing the Christmas story that a manger was a neat little place out behind the inn. Is it actually an animal feeding trough?**

. . . and she gave birth to her first son. Because there were no rooms left in the inn, she wrapped the baby with pieces of cloth and laid him in a box where animals are fed. Luke 2:7

■ **What is one sure-fire way of coming closer to the Lord?**

The LORD is close to everyone who prays to him, to all who truly pray to him. Psalm 145:18

■ **How did Jesus prove to people that He was the Messiah?**

Jesus answered . . . . "The miracles I do in my Father's name show who I am." John 10:25

■ **The shortest verse in the Bible is John 11:35, "Jesus cried." What was it that made Jesus cry?**

Part of the idea behind this book is that it will spark your interest to open the only book that gives life. Take a moment and look up the interesting answer.

■ **How important is it to tell our family members how to obtain everlasting life? I was thinking about the great flood and how only eight people in the whole earth were saved through it. Did you know those eight people were all from the same family?!**

On that same day Noah and his wife, his sons Shem, Ham, and Japheth, and their wives went into the boat. Genesis 7:13

■ **The world and life go on day in and day out. Will this go on forever or is there going to be a "last day" someday?**

"There is a judge for those who refuse to believe in me [Jesus] and do not accept my words. The word I have taught will be their judge on the last day." John 12:48

On that last day God is going to judge solely by what's in the Bible. There is no better reason why you shouldn't know your Bible inside out.

■ **Can the devil persuade you to turn against Jesus?**

The devil had already persuaded Judas Iscariot, the son of Simon, to turn against Jesus. John 13:2

Yes! Yes! Yes! That's his main job and he is very good at it.

■ **How do you protect yourself from the devil and his demons?**

Our fight is not against people on earth but against the rulers and authorities and the powers of this world's darkness, against the spiritual powers of evil in the heavenly world. That is why you need to put on God's full armor. Then on the day of evil you will be able to stand strong. And when you have finished the whole fight, you will still be standing. So stand strong, with the belt of truth tied around your waist and the protection of right living on your chest. On your feet wear the Good News of peace to help you stand strong. And also use the shield of faith with which you can stop all the burning arrows of the evil one.

Accept God's salvation as your helmet, and take the sword of the Spirit, which is the word of God. Ephesians 6:12-17

God is your source of protection. In this verse God prescribes spiritual armor so that you may stand strong against the devil's attacks.

■ **Do you suppose that of all the different religions and their holy books there must be at least 100 different ways to God?**

Jesus answered, "I am the way, and the truth, and the life. The only way to the Father [God] is through me." John 14:6

■ **So then for the people who don't believe in Jesus how do they get to God?**

Jesus answered, "I am the way, and the truth, and the life. The only way to the Father [God] is through me." John 14:6

I emphasized that verse to make the picture absolutely clear. Anyone who doesn't believe in Jesus will never know God, nor go to heaven. If that doesn't sound fair then take up the challenge and search the Scriptures to see if they are true.

■ **This is a question only Norwegians may understand. What is the ultimate "uff da?"**

"But Abraham said, 'Child, remember when you were alive you had the good things in life, but bad things happened to Lazarus. Now he is comforted here [heaven], and you are suffering [in hell]." Luke 16:25

The ultimate "uff da" is not making it to heaven. To help non-Norwegians understand the term "uff da" I will attempt to explain it through an illustration. The cat drags in a mostly dead snake and you get up in the middle of the night and step on it—that's "uff da." (Remember that, Bob?)

■ **The old real estate axiom is, "Location, location, location." When applied to your eternal home does it become paramount in importance to you? Buy the wrong line and you are stuck with the meanest slumlord for eternity!**

Dear children, do not let anyone lead you the wrong way. I John 3:7

Talking about location, Dr. D. James Kennedy, author and speaker, has located hell. He says it's at the end of a Christless life.

■ **If you love Jesus, is it guaranteed that God the Father will love you?**

". . . and my Father will love those who love me [Jesus]." John 14:21

■ **How can you tell if you really love Jesus?**

"Those who know my commands and obey them are the ones who love me [Jesus] . . . ." John 14:21a

■ **One of the Godhead is called the Helper. Who is He?**

"This Helper is the Holy Spirit whom the Father will send in my name." John 14:26

■ **What would be the greatest demonstration of love a person could show another?**

"The greatest love a person can show is to die for his friends." John 15:13

I believe this verse is talking about people in general, but most of all it's about the One who died on Good Friday for you.

■ **Who invented sex?**

God blessed them and said, "Have many children . . . ." Genesis 1:27

Is condom sense better than common sense? Is abstinence safe sex or is a condom safe sex? Did you know:
- *Condoms fail twelve percent of the time to prevent pregnancy?*
- *Condoms have naturally occurring holes that are 5 to 50 microns in diameter?*

- *The HIV virus that causes AIDS is only 0.1 micron in diameter and can pass easily through imperfections in condoms?*

- *That at a conference on AIDS 800 health experts were asked if, using a condom, they would have sex with someone who had AIDS and not one raised their hand?*[3]

■ **Jesus thinks of you as His friend. Pretty awesome thought, isn't it? Do you think of Jesus as your friend?**

"But I call you friends, because I have made known to you everything I heard from my Father." John 15:15

■ **Where does Jesus want you to be and what does He want you to see?**

"Father, I want these people that you gave me to be with me where I am [heaven]. I want them to see my glory . . . ." John 17:24

■ **Quite possibly many of you feel you weren't dealt a fair hand in this life, i.e., major physical problems, mental disorders, etc. Maybe you wanted to be a missionary in Hawaii and are confused about why you have to serve in North Pole, Alaska. We should accept the fact that God plans our steps and He made us like we are for a purpose. Shouldn't you blossom where you are planted, no matter what the circumstances are?**

Jesus said to Peter, "Put your sword back. Shouldn't I drink the cup the Father gave me?" John 18:11

■ **Are you in a religion or organization that does things in secret? Did Jesus do things in secret?**

Jesus answered, ". . . I never said anything in secret." John 18:20

■ **What did the Jews say their reason was for wanting Jesus crucified?**

The Jews answered, "We have a law that says he should die, because he said he is the Son of God." John 19:7

■ **Did Jesus actually die on the Cross?**

But when the soldiers came to Jesus and saw that he was already dead, they did not break his legs. But one of the soldiers stuck his spear into Jesus' side, and at once blood and water came out. John 19:33, 34

It is asserted by some that Jesus was indeed crucified, but that He did not actually die. They overlook one critical point. When a person dies their blood separates out the water.

■ **Is everything Jesus did while He was on earth recorded in the New Testament?**

There are many other things Jesus did. If every one of them were written down, I suppose the whole world would not be big enough for all the books that would be written. John 21:25

■ **One gift the Holy Spirit gave some believers was the ability to speak in tongues. Was that some kind of gibberish or a foreign language?**

They were all filled with the Holy Spirit, and they began to speak different languages by the power the Holy Spirit was giving them. There were some religious Jews staying in Jerusalem who were from every country in the world. When they heard this noise, a crowd came together. They were all surprised, because each one heard them speaking in his own language. Acts 2:4-6

■ **Are the promises in the Bible just for people to whom it was written or spoken to at the time?**

"This promise is for you, for your children, and for all who are far away. It is for everyone the Lord our God calls to himself." Acts 2:39

■ **Isn't it ironic that the name people use in vain, if used properly, could get them into heaven?**

"Jesus is the only One who can save people. His name is the only power in the world that has been given to save people. We must be saved through him." Acts 4:12

■ You can be safe talking about God in a group of people, but can you mention that Jesus is the only way to heaven without stirring emotions?

"But to keep it from spreading among the people, we must warn them not to talk to people anymore using that name [Jesus]." Acts 4:17

■ Should the lack of training or education keep you from spreading the Good News?

The Jewish leaders saw that Peter and John were not afraid to speak, and they understood that these men had no special training or education. So they were amazed. Acts 4:13

If my former English teachers knew I was writing they would have a good laugh. I hated English class and I have my grades to prove it. I attended the University of North Dakota and in order to graduate, a theme paper on a surprise topic was required at the end of all your studies to prove your literacy. I worried about receiving a passing grade on that paper for four years. Whether I can write well or not isn't the important spiritual point. God wants us to witness with the knowledge and skill we have and then it's the Holy Spirit's work to save the people who have been witnessed to. The next verse fits me because once the truth of the Bible was known I couldn't keep it to myself.

"We cannot keep quiet. We must speak about what we have seen and heard." Acts 4:20

■ Is Christ, Jesus' last name?

"Jesus is your holy servant, the One you made to be the Christ." Acts 4:27

Christ means Messiah—it is not His last name. A clearer way of saying His name when both names are used together is Jesus, the Christ.

■ In Hebrew, the original language of the Old Testament, God's name is JHWH. In order to pronounce it two vowels were added making it JaHWeH. What is God the Father's name in English?

Moses said to God, "When I go to the Israelites, I will say to them, 'The God of your fathers sent me to you.' What if the people say, 'What is his name?' What should I tell them." Then God said to Moses, "I AM WHO I AM. When you go to the people of Israel, tell them, 'I AM sent me to you.' " Exodus 3:13, 14

■ **What is God's title?**

Then God said to Moses, "I am the LORD." Exodus 6:2

■ **Jesus' name in Hebrew is Yeshua. What is His name in English? It's Jesus—just wanted to see if you were still alert.**

Who is the God and founder of Christianity? It's Jesus of Nazareth. Who is the God of: Baha'i, Zen Buddhists, Christian Science, Church of Jesus Christ of Latter-day Saints, Hinduism, Islam, Jehovah's Witnesses, Krishna, Metaphysical, Religious Science, Unitarian and Unity? It's definitely NOT Jesus of Nazareth.

The foundation of Christianity is that Jesus is God. Each and every other religion does not believe Jesus is God. And so they worship a false god who is different from the God (Jesus) of the Bible.

■ **What makes the Bible critically unique? It foretells future events, and this sets it apart from all other religious writings! The Bible tells history in advance multitudes of times. All other religious writings combined don't do this even once. For this to be really big news and to confirm that God inspired the Biblical writings, all events the prophets predicted to happen in the future would have to come true 100% of the time, and they have. If you have ever doubted the authenticity of the Scriptures, use Bible prophecy to bury those doubts. Let's look at some of these prophecies. Keep in mind these were written down long before they would be fulfilled.**

Prophecy—The LORD himself will give you a sign: The virgin will be pregnant. She will have a son and she will name him Immanuel. Isaiah 7:14

Fulfillment—While Joseph thought about these things, an angel of the Lord came to him in a dream. The angel said, "Joseph, descendant of

David, don't be afraid to take Mary as your wife, because the baby in her is from the Holy Spirit . . . ." All this happened to bring about what the Lord had said through the prophet: "The virgin will be pregnant. She will have a son, and they will name him Immanuel," which means "God is with us." Matthew 1:20, 22, 23

Prophecy—"But you, Bethlehem Ephrathah, though you are too small to be among the army groups from Judah, from you will come one who will rule Israel for me. He comes from very old times, from days long ago." Micah 5:2

Fulfillment—While they were in Bethlehem, the time came for Mary to have the baby, and she gave birth to her first son. Luke 2:6, 7

Prophecy—He was beaten down and punished, but he didn't say a word. He was like a lamb being led to be killed. He was quiet, as a sheep is quiet while its wool is being cut; he never opened his mouth. Isaiah 53:7

Fulfillment—Then the high priest stood up and said to Jesus, "Aren't you going to answer? Don't you have something to say about their charges against you?" But Jesus said nothing. Matthew 26:62, 63

■ **With all the evidence available wouldn't you have to call someone foolish for not believing there is a God?**

Fools say to themselves, "There is no God." Psalm 14:1

■ **The apostles, including Peter, all denied they knew Jesus when the Romans arrested Him prior to His crucifixion. Then a few weeks later all the apostles were out preaching as hard as they could about Jesus being the Messiah. What did these men see with their own eyes that dramatically changed their lives?**

With great power the apostles were telling people that the Lord Jesus was truly raised from the dead. Acts 4:33

■ **If it's the Lord's will, can He dispatch an angel to get you out of serious trouble?**

They took the apostles and put them in jail. But during the night, an angel of the Lord opened the doors of the jail and led the apostles outside. Acts 5:18, 19

■ **If the need arises can an angel speak directly to you?**

Then the angel told him, "Get dressed and put on your sandals." And Peter did. Then the angel said, "Put on your coat and follow me." Acts 12:8

■ **You've probably heard dramatic stories of people needing immediate help. Miraculously, someone helped and when the person in need turned to thank them they were nowhere to be found. Is that characteristic of a helping angel?**

They went past the first and second guards and came to the iron gate that separated them from the city. The gate opened by itself for them, and they went through it. When they had walked down one street, the angel suddenly left him. Acts 12:10

■ **What other names is Lucifer known by?**

The giant dragon was thrown down out of heaven. (He is that old snake called the devil or Satan, who tricks the whole world.) The dragon with his angels was thrown down to the earth. Revelation 12:9

There are three high ranking angels mentioned in the Scriptures. Two are good and one is evil. They are Michael, Gabriel, and Lucifer. I find these numbers interesting because when Lucifer rebelled and was cast out of heaven one third of all the angels chose to go with him. This means there are two good angels for each evil one.

■ **If man's law goes against God's law, which do you obey?**

Peter and the other apostles answered, "We must obey God, not human authority!" Acts 5:29

■ **The most important question of all questions is, "Have you accepted Jesus Christ as your Lord and Savior?" Would you agree** this may be the second most important question, "Do you have a true knowledge of God?"

People did not think it was important to have a true knowledge of God. So God left them and allowed them to have their own worthless thinking and to do things they should not do. Romans 1:28

■ **If you suffer disgrace for Jesus, what should your emotional state of mind be?**

They called the apostles in, beat them, and told them not to speak in the name of Jesus again. Then they let them go free. The apostles left the meeting full of joy because they were given the honor of suffering disgrace for Jesus. Acts 5:40, 41

■ **When trying to convince someone that Jesus is the only way to heaven, might some of the words come to you directly from the Holy Spirit?**

They all came and argued with Stephen. But the Spirit was helping him to speak with wisdom, and his words were so strong that they could not argue with him. Acts 6:9, 10

■ **Does your status in life affect the way you think of yourself?**

"I really understand now that to God every person is the same." Acts 10:34

Some people have terribly low self-esteem while others have puffed up egos. What God thinks about us is extremely more important than how we view ourselves. That is very good news for low self-esteem, but will be tough on that ego.

■ **Interestingly, today we don't think of Jewish people as Christians, but in the early church weren't the first Christians Jewish?**

Many of the believers . . . went as far as Phoenicia, Cyprus, and Antioch telling the message to others, but only to Jews. Acts 11:19

Yes, the early Christian church consisted mainly of Jews.

■ **Do Christians and turkey have anything in common? In what city and country were believers first called Christians?**

In Antioch [Turkey] the followers were called Christians for the first time. Acts 11:26

■ **Do we have our priorities mixed up much of the time? In reality life is very short, so why do we knock ourselves out trying to accumulate stuff that in a brief time will belong to someone else?**

You have given me only a short life; my lifetime is like nothing to you. Everyone's life is only a breath. People are like shadows moving about. All their work is for nothing; they collect things but don't know who will get them. "So, LORD, what hope do I have? You are my hope. Save me from all my sins." Psalm 39:5-8

■ **Isn't it odd for people who don't believe in God to use His name as a swear word? Why should we treat God's name with utmost respect?**

He is holy and wonderful. Psalm 111:9

You must not use the name of the LORD your God thoughtlessly; the LORD will punish anyone who misuses his name. Exodus 20:7

■ **Does Israel belong to the Palestinians or the Jews? Who did God give the land to?**

God . . . gave the land [Israel] to his people [the Jews]. Acts 13:19

■ **Several thousand years ago it was predicted there would be trouble in the Holy Land just prior to the Second Coming of Jesus. The current turbulence has been over the entire territory of Israel, but which city will become the focal point of the trouble?**

I will make Jerusalem like a cup of poison to the nations around her. They will come and attack Jerusalem . . . . Zachariah 12:2

■ An easy way to recognize that the Jews are God's chosen people is by analyzing this question: What two groups of people make up the world's population?

. . . whether we are Jews or Gentiles . . . . Romans 9:24 TLB

■ Because the Jews are chosen, does that make them special?

The LORD says, "People of Jacob, you are my servants. Listen to me! People of Israel, I chose you." Isaiah 44:1

Are the Jews any more special than you or I? Not really because you can categorize people another way—saved or unsaved. Then why are the Jews God's chosen people? They are the apple of God's eye plus He chose them to write and preserve the Holy Scriptures. They were also chosen to bring forth the Messiah from their nationality.

■ King David was a great man, but he was also an adulterer and a murderer. After David asked forgiveness for those sins did God say, "You are forgiven, but you are not exactly the type of person I am looking for?"

" . . . God made David their king. God said about him: 'I have found in David son of Jesse the kind of man I want.' " Acts 13:22

David was sorry for his sin and asked for forgiveness thus allowing God to use him. You can't be any worse than David, therefore you are the kind of person God wants too. He will forgive you for anything you have done. Yes, anything!

■ They used to preach about Jesus in the synagogue. What happened?

But Paul and Barnabas spoke very boldly, saying, "We must speak the message of God [Jesus] to you [the Jews] first. But you refuse to listen." Acts 13:46

■ Do you have to be born Jewish to be in the Jewish religion?

When the meeting was over, many Jews and those who had changed to the Jewish religion . . . . Acts 13:43

■ **Is "the Church" a building or a group of people?**

When they arrived in Antioch, Paul and Barnabas gathered the church together. They told the church all about what God had done with them and how God had made it possible for those who were not Jewish to believe. Acts 14:27

Christians make up "the Church".

■ **Shouldn't it have been relatively easy for the Jews of Jesus time to figure out from the Old Testament Scriptures that He was the Messiah?**

Paul went into the synagogue as he always did, and on each Sabbath day for three weeks, he talked with the Jews about the [Old Testament] Scriptures. He explained and proved that the Christ [Messiah] must die and then rise from the dead. He said, "This Jesus I am telling you about is the Christ." Acts 17:2, 3

■ **Shouldn't it be relatively easy for the Jews of our time to figure out Jesus is the Messiah?**

He [Apollos] argued very strongly with the Jews before all the people, clearly proving with the Scriptures [Old Testament] that Jesus is the Christ. Acts 18:28

Yes, they could understand who the Messiah is but like so many, both Jew and Gentile, they fail to study the life giving Scriptures.

■ **Salvation of your soul is the greatest of God's Good News. What might be the second best thing about God's Good News?**
. . . the Good News about God's grace. Acts 20:24

■ **Will there be a day we won't argue over whether God exists or not?**

We will all stand before God to be judged, because it is written in the Scriptures: " 'As surely as I live,' says the Lord, 'Everyone will bow before me; everyone will say that I am God.' " Romans 14:10, 11

■ **You can't work or buy your way into heaven because Jesus has already paid your way. Was the price paid in full with His blood and suffering?**

. . . the church of God, which he bought with the death of his own son. Acts 20:28

■ **Can women prophesy or is that for the men of the church?**

He had four unmarried daughters who had the gift of prophesying. Acts 21:9

■ **Why do fellow Christians call each other brother and sister?**

Then they said to Paul, "Brother, you can see that many thousands of Jews have become believers." Acts 21:20

It's because believers are in the family of God. God is the Father and we are His children. Hence, we are brothers and sisters.

■ **Did Paul, who wrote much of the New Testament, beat and persecute Christians before he was saved?**

"I [Paul] persecuted the people who followed the Way of Jesus, and some of them were even killed. I arrested men and women and put them in jail." Acts 22:4

Once people turn to the Lord for salvation, God puts their past behind them. If you want a new beginning and a new life, accept Jesus as Savior and Lord.

■ **If you mistreat Christians, is it the same as mistreating Jesus?**

"Saul, why are you persecuting me?" I asked, "Who are you Lord?" The voice said, "I am Jesus of Nazareth, whom you are persecuting." Acts 22:7, 8

Paul's name was Saul before he became a Christian. At the time of this verse Jesus was in heaven so Paul was persecuting Jesus by mistreating Christians.

■ **Was capital punishment dreamed up by man or ordained by God?**

. . . I [God] will demand the life of anyone who takes another person's life. Genesis 9:5

Capital punishment works because it deters crime. Every murderer executed has never killed again!

■ **Does capital punishment conflict with the sixth commandment as it is commonly quoted from the King James version, "Thou shalt not kill?"**

"You must not <u>murder</u> [emphasis added] anyone." Exodus 20:13 New Century Version

The Old Testament was translated from Hebrew to English and a much more accurate meaning is derived with a clear translation. It then becomes evident that capital punishment is not in conflict with the sixth commandment.

■ **Most pictures I see show just two of each animal going into Noah's ark. Is that accurate?**

Take with you [Noah] seven pairs, each male with its female, of every kind of clean animal, and take one pair, each male with its female, of every kind of unclean animal. Take seven pairs of all the birds of the sky . . . . Genesis 7:2, 3

■ **How in the world did Noah and his family gather up all those animals?**

The clean animals, the unclean animals, the birds, and everything that crawls on the ground came to Noah. Genesis 7:8, 9

When God asks you to do something, He is there to help.

■ **Does the Rapture occur before, during or at the end of the Tribulation period? What are "types" in Scripture and can they help solve this question?**

He [Noah] and his wife and his sons and their wives went into the boat to escape the waters of the flood. Seven days later the flood started. Genesis 7:7, 10

There is a controversy as to when the Rapture of the Church to heaven takes place. The ideal time is just before chaos breaks loose on earth prior to the seven year Tribulation period. One very interesting technique used in the Scriptures is called "types." In the above Scripture Noah and his family, I believe, are a type of the end-time Church. They went into the safety of the Ark seven days <u>before</u> the great flood. I say that's an insightful clue that during the seven years of tribulation we Christians will be in the safety of heaven.

Now if you just said, "Mike, that is really stretching things.", then consider these other "types." There was only one door into the ark— there is only one door into heaven. "I [Jesus] am the door, and the person who enters through me will be saved . . . ." (John 10:9). There was only one ark to escape death—there is only one Jesus to save you from death. That means the members of all cults and liberal churches who have a different Jesus than the Jesus of the New Testament won't make it into heaven! Now if I just upset you by saying that, I beg you to thoroughly check this out. I suggest you contact the Christian Research Institute. They have free fact sheets on most religious organizations to help you. Address: PO Box 7000, Rancho Santa Margarita, CA 92688-7000.

■ **I personally like the idea of being raptured. I believe with all my heart we are that generation of believers who will be taken to heaven without experiencing death. There were two individuals in the Old Testament who were "raptured." This gives me confidence that the Rapture we talk about in our day is not something new and strange. Who were these two people that never died and do they represent a "type" of anything?**

Enoch walked with God; one day Enoch could not be found, because God took him. Genesis 5:24

As they were walking and talking, a chariot and horses of fire appeared and separated Elijah from Elisha. Then Elijah went up to heaven in a whirlwind. II Kings 2:11

These men are a "type" of Rapture for New Testament believers. Just like Enoch and Elijah were caught up to heaven, so will Christians living in the end times be caught up to heaven alive in the Rapture.

■ **If a church or religion has another book or teaching they claim is equal to or held in higher esteem than the Bible, such as the Book of Mormon, teachings from the Watchtower, and etc., do they serve a different Jesus than the Jesus of the Bible? I don't want anyone to miss this one so I am going to give you the first three letters of the correct answer. Y—E—S.**

Anyone who goes beyond Christ's teaching and does not continue to follow only his teaching does not have God. II John 9

What do I mean when I say they serve a different Jesus? Cults and false religions use Bible names and terminology, but they have substituted their own meanings for them. The religions I mentioned above do not believe Jesus is God! Hence, they worship another Jesus and as the verse said they do not have God!

■ **Do you want to be happy? Do you want to enjoy what you work for? Do you want to be blessed with good things? Here's how.**

Happy are those who respect the LORD and obey Him. You will enjoy what you work for, and you will be blessed with good things. Psalm 128:1, 2

■ **Did Adam and Eve have belly buttons?**

Then God said, "Let us make human beings in our image and likeness." Genesis 1:26

My wife, who is doing the computer work for this book, mentioned she read where dogs have belly buttons. We had never thought of that. The article did say they are concealed pretty well. We have a cute little dog named Sioux and her belly button is so well concealed we couldn't find it. I feel it is a testimony to their creation that Adam and Eve did not have belly buttons.

■ **Christians are grateful God forgives us of _everything_, but do we have to forgive others of _everything_?**

"When you are praying, if you are angry with someone, forgive him so that your Father in heaven will also forgive your sins. But if you don't forgive other people, then your Father in heaven will not forgive your sins." Mark 11:25, 26

Just a brief truth like this could change your life. If you are full of bitterness and anger towards someone, forgive them right now and see how much your quality of life improves.

■ **Do you wonder, when praying, if and how God actually hears your prayers?**

Where can I go to get away from your Spirit? Where can I run from you? If I go up to the heavens, you are there. If I lie down in the grave, you are there. If I rise with the sun in the east and settle in the west beyond the sea, even there you would guide me. Psalm 139:7-10

He hears (even silent prayers) because He is omnipresent. That means He is everywhere at the same time and near to hear your prayers. How can God be everywhere at the same time? He is Spirit and has no physical limitations.

■ **What does the word omniscient mean?**

LORD . . . You know my thoughts before I think them. You know where I go and where I lie down. You know thoroughly everything I do. LORD, even before I say a word, you already know it [emphasis added]. Psalm 139:1-4

Omniscient means all knowing.

■ **The word gospel means Good News. Who is the Good News about?**

The Good News is about God's Son, Jesus Christ our Lord. Romans 1:3

■ **What do you think of gay marriages? Are you for, against, or just neutral?**

Homosexuality is absolutely forbidden, for it is an enormous sin. Leviticus 18:22

I suspect Christians who don't take a firm stand against this either attend a liberal church or they just flat don't know what the Word of God says.

■ **Is it unnatural and shameful to have sex with someone of the same gender?**

Because people did those things, God left them and let them do the shameful things they wanted to do. Women stopped having natural sex and started having sex with other women. In the same way, men stopped having natural sex and began wanting each other. Romans 1:26, 27

■ **If you practice homosexual sex, is it likely you are going to catch some disease you don't want?**

Men did shameful things with other men, and in their bodies they received the punishment for those wrongs. Romans 1:27

If God's Word is true then statistics and facts should back up the statement, "in their bodies they received the punishment for those wrongs."
- *Homosexuals are 23 times more likely than a heterosexual to contract a sexually transmitted disease.*
- *78% of homosexuals have a sexually transmitted disease.*
- *50% of the gay population in the world have gonorrhea.*
- *Homosexuals carry half of the nation's syphilis.*
- *The life expectancy of a gay male is only 42 years of age.*
- *Only 3% of America's homosexuals are 55 years old or older.*
- *Less than 1% of homosexuals dies of old age.* [4]

Does God hate homosexuals? Quite the contrary is true. God loves all people so much He sent Jesus to die for their sins.

■ **How did homosexuality start in the first place? Are people born that way?**

They traded the glory of God who lives forever for the worship of idols made to look like earthly people, birds, animals, and snakes. Because they did these things, God left them and let them go their sinful way, wanting only to do evil. As a result, they became full of sexual sin, using their bodies wrongly with each other. Romans 1:23, 24

People are not born that way. Homosexuality is a result of a voluntary decision to do what they want to do without regard for God's will. If homosexuals were born that way God could not condemn homosexuality as a sin! Many people in this lifestyle were abused as children and get confused about their sexuality. For them it is very difficult to know what's right. That's why they must rely on the only source of truth, the Holy Bible, for black and white answers.

■ **I say it is impossible to be an atheist. What do you say?**

For the truth about God is known to them instinctively; God has put this knowledge in their hearts. Since earliest times men have seen the earth and sky and all God made, and have known of his existence and great eternal power. So they will have no excuse [when they stand before God at Judgment Day]. Romans 1:19, 20 TLB

■ **Is a person's nature derived from his beliefs? These verses answer why humans are so depraved, why some people treat others so badly and why people do such ugly things to fellow humans.**

People did not think it was important to have a true knowledge of God. So God left them and allowed them to have their own worthless thinking and to do things they should not do. They are filled with every kind of sin, evil, selfishness, and hatred. They are full of jealousy, murder, fighting, lying, and thinking the worst about each other. They gossip and say evil things about each other. They hate God. They are rude and conceited and brag about themselves. They invent ways of doing evil. They do not obey their parents. They are foolish, they do not keep their promises, and they show no kindness or mercy to others. They know God's law says that those who live like this should die. But they themselves not only continue to do these evil things, they applaud others who do them. Romans 1:28-32

Chapter Six

**"To read the Bible is to take a trip to a fair land
where the spirit is strengthened and faith renewed."**
- Dwight D. Eisenhower -

■ **Will your eternal home be much better or much worse than your present home?**

But our homeland is in heaven, and we are waiting for our Savior, the Lord Jesus Christ, to come from heaven. Philippians 3:20

And anyone whose name was not found written in the book of life was thrown into the lake of fire. Revelation 20:15

I like how Dave Breese, host of the Dave Breese Report, expressed his world view. He stated, "If you are a Christian this world is the worst you will experience, but if you are not a Christian then this world is the best you will experience."

■ **Is tomorrow going to be pretty much like today?**

". . . a quart of wheat for a day's pay, and three quarts of barley for a day's pay . . . ." Revelation 6:6

Most of us probably assumes each day will be similar to the next, but compare December 6, 1941, to December 7, 1941, the day the Japanese bombed Pearl Harbor. In March of 1997 the country of Albania was in chaos because most of the population invested in a get rich quick scheme that robbed the people of their savings. As I was watching the carnage in Albania on TV the thought hit me that this is the way it will

*be in the United States during the Tribulation period.   Your
neighborhood could be like a battle zone with crazed people looking for
food and money.   This will be brought on in part by near financial
collapse with inflation running rampant.   Imagine working a full day
just to buy a loaf of bread.   Good news! All serious followers of the true
Jesus will not be on earth during this terrible time.*

■ **Is it humanly possible to keep the Ten Commandments and gain heaven that way?**

. . . because no one can be made right with God by following the law.
Romans 3:20

■ **So what is the purpose of the law and the commandments today?**

The law only shows us our sin. Romans 3:20b

■ **How do you get right with God if following His law doesn't do it?**

But God has a way to make people right with him without the law, and
he has now shown us that way which the law and the prophets told us
about. God makes people right with himself through their faith in Jesus
Christ. Romans 3:21, 22

■ **How are you made free from sin?**

They need to be made free from sin through Jesus Christ. God gave him
as a way to forgive sin through faith in the blood of Jesus' death.
Romans 3:24, 25

*Are you noticing everything centers and focuses on Jesus?   I like
alerting people to clues about the churches they attend. If your church
doesn't mention Jesus much you are in grave spiritual danger!*

■ **Does God always do what is right?**

This showed that God always does what is right and fair . . . . Romans
3:25

■ **There are numerous unfavorable situations that come our way. How are we to understand why these things happen to us?**

Since the Lord is directing our steps, why try to understand everything that happens along the way? Proverbs 20:24 TLB

■ **Who is the most respected Jew and father of the Jews?**

So what can we say that Abraham, the father of our people [the Jews] . . . . Romans 4:1

■ **Should the truth of Scripture set people free from misinformation? Many people are burdened with the theology that they have to perform tasks or good deeds to be made right with God. Well, here is a solid black and white answer to that.**

But people cannot do any work that will make them right with God. So they must trust in him, who makes even evil people right in his sight. Then God accepts their faith, and that makes them right with him. David said the same thing. He said that people are truly blessed when God, without paying attention to good deeds, makes people right with himself. Romans 4:5, 6

■ **What percent of the world's population always does what is right?**

There is no one who always does what is right, not even one. Romans 3:10

■ **Happiness is something we all search for and some long for. Shouldn't the creator of happiness be able to give us some pointers in achieving this precious state?**

Happy are they whose sins are forgiven, whose wrongs are pardoned. Happy is the person who the Lord does not consider guilty. Romans 4:7, 8

This verse is conditional. You must ask for forgiveness first, then the promise of happiness is yours.

■ At some point God's anger is going to be poured out on this sin-filled world. You certainly want to avoid that, but how do you accomplish it?

So through Christ we will surely be saved from God's anger because we have been made right with God by the blood of Christ's death. Romans 5:9

This verse is conditional too. Your part is to accept Christ as your Lord and Savior, then God's promise of avoiding His anger is yours.

■ Having friends is very important. Wouldn't the ultimate be to have God as your friend?

. . . but now we are also very happy in God through our Lord Jesus Christ. Through him we are now God's friends again. Romans 5:11

■ Where did sin come from?

Sin came into the world because of what one man [Adam] did, and with sin came death. This is why everyone must die—because everyone sinned. Romans 5:12

Because one man sinned we all have to die. But because one man [Jesus] died, we can all live again!

So as one sin of Adam brought the punishment of death to all people, one good act that Christ did makes all people right with God. And that brings true life for all. Romans 5:18

■ The physical body wears out and dies, but what brings death to a person's spirit?

You can follow sin, which brings spiritual death, or you can obey God, which makes you right with him. Romans 6:16

If you are born once, you die twice. If you are born twice, you die once. If that made sense, you are an excellent Bible student. You are born and die physically and your spirit is either born again or it dies.

They reject God's authority .... So they are twice dead. Jude 8, 12

■ **Earning excellent dividends is good, but what dividends does sin pay?**

When people sin, they earn what sin pays—death. Romans 6:23

■ **How much money do you have to pay to obtain eternal life?**

But God gives us a free gift—life forever in Christ Jesus our Lord. Romans 6:23

That may have seemed like a simple question, but you wouldn't believe the number of people in organized faiths that believe spiritual favor is gained by paying money to the Church.

■ **Were the people God used to write down the Scriptures "holier than thou" kind of people?**

"I do not understand the things I do. I do not do what I want to do, and I do the things I hate." Romans 7:15

Just like nearly all the people of the Bible, these individuals were just typical and tempted by sin like you and I. The writer was the apostle Paul and he said these things about himself.

■ **What makes us do the things we know we shouldn't do?**

But I [Paul, the apostle] am not really the one who is doing these hated things; it is sin living in me that does them. Romans 7:17

■ **What is just one of many ways to test yourself to see if you really are a child of God?**

The true children of God are those who let God's Spirit lead them. Romans 8:14

■ **Do you get discouraged because you wish you could express yourself better in prayer? Well, be discouraged no more.**

Also the Spirit helps us with our weakness. We do not know how to pray as we should. But the Spirit himself speaks to God for us, even begs God for us with deep feelings that words cannot explain. God can see what is in people's hearts. And he knows what is in the mind of the Spirit, because the Spirit speaks to God for his people in the way God wants. Romans 8:26, 27

■ **If you are a self-made millionaire or financially well off don't get too puffed up that you did it all by yourself. Who may have blessed you?**

You might say to yourself, "I am rich because of my own power and strength," but remember the LORD your God! It is he who gives you the power to become rich . . . . Deuteronomy 8:17, 18

■ **How can Christians be sure they will never be defeated by the devil?**

If God is with us, no one can defeat us. Romans 8:31

Deposit this verse in your heart, you will have to draw on it occasionally.

■ **I believe the end of the present age is close at hand. To understand God's time clock we have to look and see what He is doing with His chosen people, the Jews, and their land, Israel. Will the generation that sees Jerusalem back in Jewish hands be the final generation before the Lord returns to take his people to heaven?**

"And Jerusalem will be trampled by Gentiles until the times of the Gentiles are fulfilled [June 7, 1967, the day the Jews retook control of Jerusalem, this prophecy was fulfilled] . . . . Assuredly, I say to you, this generation will by no means pass away till all things are fulfilled." Luke 21:24, 32 NKJV

How long is a generation? There has been a lot of speculation on this question, but if we let Scripture answer our questions we will have a solid answer. The Lord, when talking of a generation of people, pinpoints 38 years!

"And the time we took to come from Kadesh Barnea until we crossed over the Valley of the Zered was thirty-eight years, until all the generation of the men of war was consumed from the midst of the camp, just as the LORD had sworn to them." Deuteronomy 2:14 NKJV

■ **If you believe in Christ, who is your conscience ruled by?**

I am in Christ, and I am telling you the truth; I do not lie. My conscience is ruled by the Holy Spirit. Romans 9:1

■ **How does your mouth play a role in attaining heaven?**

If you use your mouth to say, "Jesus is Lord" and if you believe in your heart that God raised Jesus from the dead, you will be saved. We believe with our hearts, and so we are made right with God. And we use our mouths to say that we believe, and so we are saved. Romans 10:9, 10

■ **Are you hesitant about trusting in Jesus? Don't be. You can bank on this exciting promise made to you personally.**

As the Scripture says, "Anyone who trusts in him will never be disappointed." Romans 10:11

■ **Do you consider your pastor to be beautiful?**

It is written, "How beautiful is the person who comes to bring good news." Romans 10:15

■ **Can you use Miracle-Gro® to make your faith grow?**

So faith comes from hearing the Good News, and people hear the Good News when someone tells them about Christ. Romans 10:17

As a suggestion to make your faith grow, put on a portable cassette player with exciting Christian teaching tapes and listen to them while applying Miracle-Gro® to your plants. You must listen to God's Word for your faith to grow! This Scripture says "hearing," but you can "hear" about God by reading also.

■ I admire knowledgeable people. When I have a car or appliance problem I can't figure out, I'd rather call a friend who can tell me how to fix it rather than be at the mercy of people who know how to charge "primo" rates. Spiritually, you can say I've got it made because I have this one Friend who has so much wisdom and knowledge He has ALL the answers to life's most difficult circumstances. Can you name my Friend?

Yes, God's riches are very great, and his wisdom and knowledge have no end! Romans 11:33

■ Why do bad things happen to good people?

No one can explain the things God decides or understand his ways. As the Scripture says, "Who has known the mind of the Lord, or who has been able to give him advice?" Romans 11:33, 34

■ God has given you a special gift to help other people. What is your gift and is it getting used?

We all have different gifts, each of which came because of the grace God gave us. The person who has the gift of prophecy should use that gift in agreement with the faith. Anyone who has the gift of serving should serve. Anyone who has the gift of teaching should teach. Whoever has the gift of encouraging others should encourage. Whoever has the gift of giving to others should give freely. Anyone who has the gift of being a leader should try hard when he leads. Whoever has the gift of showing mercy to others should do so with joy. Romans 12:6-8

■ If evil could be defeated, do you think you could get the upper hand in this battle of life?

Do not let evil defeat you, but defeat evil by doing good. Romans 12:21

■ This is one of those difficult areas to understand, but does God allow evil politicians to be elected?

No one rules unless God has given him the power to rule, and no one rules now without that power from God. So those who are against the government are really against what God has commanded. Romans 13:1, 2

■ **Some radical anti-government groups quote the Bible but reject government authority. They also do not support paying taxes. Do you suppose their Bible reads different from mine?**

So you must yield to the government . . . . If you owe any kind of tax, pay it. Show respect and honor to them all. Romans 13:5, 7

■ **God's Word says be careful how much money you owe and to whom you owe it. However, there is one thing you should owe a lot of. What is that precious commodity?**

. . . except always owe love to each other . . . . Romans 13:8

■ **You must agree on the fundamentals of Scripture (points necessary for salvation) but never argue about non-essentials. Could you lose friends arguing?**

Accept into your group someone who is weak in faith, and do not argue about opinions. Romans 14:1

■ **Some people believe sinning ceases when a person becomes a Christian. I say it is impossible to stop totally—even when wanting to. What do you say?**

Anything that is done without believing it is right is a sin. Romans 14:23

■ **Can Jesus be found in the Old Testament?**

"Who has gone up to heaven and come back down? Who can hold the wind in his hand? Who can gather up the waters in his coat? Who has set in place the ends of the earth? What is his name or his <u>son's name</u> [emphasis added]? Tell me, if you know!" Proverbs 30:4

He was beaten down and punished, but he didn't say a word. He was like a lamb being led to be killed. He was quiet as a sheep is quiet while its wool is being cut; he never opened his mouth. Men took him away roughly and unfairly. He died without children to continue his family. He was put to death; he was punished for the sins of my people. He was buried with wicked men and he died with the rich. He had done nothing wrong, and he had never lied. Isaiah 53:7-9

Jesus himself testifies it was Him that Moses and the old Testament prophets were talking about!

Then starting with what Moses and all the prophets had said about him, Jesus began to explain everything that had been written about himself in the Scriptures. Luke 24:27

■ **Was the temple in Jerusalem replaced by your physical body?**

Don't you know that you are God's temple and that God's Spirit lives in you? If anyone destroys God's temple, God will destroy that person, because God's temple is holy and you are that temple. I Corinthians 3:16

■ **Don't get upset with me for asking this question please. If you are street smart or have a formal degree but don't know much about God; are you foolish?**

Stop fooling yourselves. If you count yourself above average in intelligence, as judged by this world's standards, you had better put this all aside and be a fool rather than let it hold you back from the true wisdom from above. For the wisdom of this world is foolishness to God. I Corinthians 3:18, 19 TLB

■ **What does yeast represent in the Bible?**

So let us celebrate this feast, but not with the bread that has the old yeast—the yeast of sin and wickedness. I Corinthians 5:8

■ **True or false? A Christian should not judge another Christian.**

But you must judge the people who are part of the church. The Scripture says, "You must get rid of the evil person among you." I Corinthians 5:13

Some things must be judged and other things should not be judged. You must judge yourself, but you cannot judge another person's intention or what is in their heart.

■ **Are angels going to judge us someday or are we going to judge them?**

You know that in the future we will judge angels, so surely we can judge the ordinary things of this life. I Corinthians 6:3

■ **The conventional question is, "How do you get into heaven?" But I ask, "What must you do to stay out of heaven?"**

Surely you know that the people who do wrong will not inherit God's kingdom. Do not be fooled. Those who sin sexually, worship idols, take part in adultery, those who are male prostitutes, or men who have sexual relations with other men, those who steal, are greedy, get drunk, lie about others, or rob—these people will not inherit God's kingdom. I Corinthians 6:9, 10

■ **Can Christians be tempted with sexual sin? Sure, but put this piece of Scripture in your memory bank and withdraw it at temptation time.**

Surely you know that your bodies are parts of Christ himself. So I must never take the parts of Christ and join them to a prostitute! I Corinthians 6:15

■ **What kind of running will keep you spiritually healthy?**

So run away from sexual sin. I Corinthians 6:18

■ **There's only one good Biblical reason why a married couple should abstain from having sexual relations, and even then it should be just for a short time. What is that prayerful reason?**

The husband should give his wife all that he owes her as his wife. And the wife should give her husband all that she owes him as her husband. The wife does not have full rights over her own body; her husband shares them. And the husband does not have full rights over his own body; his wife shares them. Do not refuse to give your bodies to each other, unless you both agree to stay away from sexual relations for a time so you can give your time to prayer. Then come together again so Satan cannot tempt you because of a lack of self-control. I Corinthians 7:3-5

■ **Is there anything wrong with being single?**

Now for those who are not married and for the widows I say this: It is good for them to stay unmarried as I [Paul, the apostle] am. I Corinthians 7:8

There is nothing wrong with being single. The reason I am mentioning this is because some singles are put on a guilt trip by people who are not familiar with the Bible.

■ **Do you think you aren't worth much? Hogwash! Who told you that? It must have been the devil or your own mind thought that fiction up.**

You all were bought at a great price [the crucifixion at Calvary] . . . . I Corinthians 7:23

■ **Your temptations are not unique, and you cannot be tempted more than you can stand. It's just pure nonsense to say, "The devil made me do it." Does God always give a way out of temptation?**

The only temptation that has come to you is that which everyone has. But you can trust God, who will not permit you to be tempted more than you can stand. But when you are tempted, he will also give you a way to escape so that you will be able to stand it. I Corinthians 10:13

■ **Who, besides the bank, really owns your house and car?**

". . . because the earth belongs to the Lord, and everything in it." I Corinthians 10:26

■ **In what particular instance is it OK to hurt someone?**

Never do anything that might hurt others—Jews, Greeks, or God's Church . . . . I Corinthians 10:32

This is not talking about your need to protect yourself from physical harm.

■ **Can sickness or early death occur just from taking communion?**

So if anyone eats this bread and drinks from this cup of the Lord in an unworthy manner, he is guilty of sin against the body and the blood of the Lord. That is why a man should examine himself carefully before eating the bread and drinking from the cup. For if he eats the bread and drinks from the cup unworthily, not thinking about the body of Christ and what it means, he is eating and drinking God's judgment upon himself; for he is trifling with the death of Christ. That is why many of you are weak and sick, and some have even died. I Corinthians 11:27-30 TLB

■ **Have you ever been sentenced to death? Think about this one carefully before answering.**

For the wages of sin is death, but the gift of God is eternal life in Christ Jesus our Lord. Romans 6:23 NKJV

Unless you have accepted God's gift of eternal life you still have a sentence of death upon you!

■ **Many charismatic Christians take speaking in tongues way too seriously. In the list of gifts in Corinthians it's almost last and then it's up to the Holy Spirit to assign these different gifts to whom He wants. What sense does it make to list a choice of gifts and then give the same one to everybody?**

One Spirit, the same Spirit, does all these things, and the Spirit decides what to give each person . . . . If each part of the body were the same part, there would be no body. But truly God put all the parts, each one of them, in the body as he wanted them . . . . Not all speak in different languages. Not all interpret those languages. But you should truly want to have the greater gifts. I Corinthians 12:11, 18, 19, 30, 31

■ Let's say you are really blessed and have several gifts of the Spirit. But, if you lack this one attribute, are you just a gifted dud?

But I gain nothing if I do not have love. I Corinthians 13:3

■ Love is a very encompassing word and difficult to define. God is love, so shouldn't He know best how to explain it?

Love is patient and kind. Love is not jealous, it does not brag, and it is not proud. Love is not rude, is not selfish, and does not get upset with others. Love does not count up wrongs that have been done. Love is not happy with evil but is happy with the truth. Love patiently accepts all things. It always trusts, always hopes, and always remains strong. Love never ends. I Corinthians 13:4-8

■ Speaking in tongues is actually speaking in another known language that has not been studied or learned. Could it also be a language angels speak?

I may speak in different languages of people or even angels. I Corinthians 13:1

■ If you want to know about God's will for your life in a particular situation, ask yourself, "Does this bring me peace or confusion?"

God is not a God of confusion but a God of peace. I Corinthians 14:33

Don't read this one over too fast. It's short but it's powerful. Use the concept on at least your primary decisions.

■ If all churches would use the Bible as the ONLY source of truth, wouldn't they all essentially be preaching the same thing?

So if I preached to you or the other apostles preached to you, we all preach the same thing . . . . I Corinthians 15:11

Truly, you can't know if your church is teaching abnormal theology if you don't know what's in the Book.

■ **True or false? The Christian faith is based totally on the fact that Jesus Christ rose from the dead.**

And if Christ has not been raised, then your faith has nothing to it; you are still guilty of your sins. I Corinthians 15:17

■ **Will you lift debauched individuals up to where you are or will they drag you down to where they are?**

Do not be fooled: "Bad friends will ruin good habits." I Corinthians 15:33

■ **I don't want to shake you out of your tree but if evolution were true, wouldn't all things have the same kind of flesh?**

All things made of flesh are not the same: People have one kind of flesh, animals have another, birds have another, and fish have another. I Corinthians 15:39

Have you seen the IHOP® television ad where a successful chicken producer is asked, "Which came first, the chicken or the egg?" You know his brains aren't scrambled because he is running a thriving business, but his surprising answer was, "I don't know." If he had spent just a few minutes of his lifetime in the first chapter of Genesis he could have answered "over easily" that it was the chicken.

■ **Once a person is raised from the grave, at the time Jesus returns, can his body ever die or deteriorate again?**

The body that is "planted" will ruin and decay, but it is raised to a life that cannot be destroyed. I Corinthians 15:42

When we die, as Christians, we are immediately in the presence of the Lord in our spirit bodies. With the first resurrection, at the Rapture of the Church, Christians who are alive on earth and the people in heaven receive new glorified incorruptible bodies that will last for eternity! Please repeat after me, "Hallelujah."

■ **True or False? Our new glorified resurrected body will not be made of flesh nor will it have any blood.**

I tell you this, brothers and sisters: Flesh and blood cannot have a part in the kingdom of God. Something that will ruin cannot have a part in something that never ruins. I Corinthians 15:50

■ **Is there an infinite or finite number of stars?**

The LORD . . . He counts the stars and names each one. Psalm 147:4

God has named each one so there must be a set number of them.

■ **I hope you will learn to love end-time prophecy because it is extremely fascinating. Believers that are alive when Christ returns at the Rapture will be taken to heaven without dying. That's exciting. I strongly believe we are the generation that will not have to taste death.**

But look! I tell you this secret: We will not all sleep in death, but we will all be changed. It will only take a second—as quickly as an eye blinks—when the last trumpet sounds. The trumpet will sound, and those who have died will be raised to live forever, and we [who are alive] will all be changed [receive glorified bodies]. I Corinthians 15:51, 52

What's the difference in believing this and what Heaven's Gate, a cult group near San Diego where 39 people committed suicide in 1997, had to offer? The followers of Doe should have reasoned, "You go first Doe and in three days when you rise from the dead, then we'll talk." They believed a lie from a fast talker who couldn't back up with evidence what he taught. On the other hand, Christians have the Holy Scriptures to back them up. As hard as people have tried, no one in the last two thousand years has been able to prove that even one point in any book of the Bible is false. Some of the strongest believers are people who set out to disprove the Scriptures but found the Bible to be absolutely true. The Scriptures have never been changed to line up with truth because they have never been in error! Ask a Jehovah's Witness or a Mormon how many times their official writings have been changed because of errors. To get an unbiased truthful answer to that question I suggest you ask an independent source to verify the many times their material has had to be corrected.

■ **Are you weary, frustrated, or just burned out that what you are doing for the Lord is just wasted time? Well, refresh yourself with this memory verse.**

Always give yourselves fully to the work of the Lord, because you know that your work in the Lord is never wasted. I Corinthians 15:58

■ **If you choose not to love the Lord, do you know the full ramifications of that decision?**

If anyone does not love the Lord, let him be separated from God—lost forever! I Corinthians 16:22

■ **God is in the business of saving souls and raising people from the dead. Should you have stock in this business?**

. . . God, who raises people from the dead [at the end time]. II Corinthians 1:9

■ **Are you under bondage? Well, quit it—here's how.**

The Lord is the Spirit, and where the Spirit of the Lord is, there is freedom. II Corinthians 3:17

■ **Is it ever all right to change the Word of God?**

We use no trickery, and we do not change the teaching of God. II Corinthians 4:2

Beware of teams of people who come to the door and tell you about a wonderful Jesus. The Jehovah's Witnesses and Mormons are nice enough people but they are cleverly deceived. The sad part is they talk like Christians but in fact they do not believe Jesus is God (a requirement to enter heaven). They change the sacred word of God to fit what they believe.

So I am amazed that you are turning away so quickly and believing something different than the Good News. Really, there is no other Good News. But some people are confusing you; they want to change the Good News of Christ [emphasis added]. We preached to you the Good

News. So if we ourselves, or even an angel from heaven, should preach to you something different, we should be judged guilty! . . . If anyone is preaching something different to you, he should be judged guilty! Galatians 1:6-9

Guess which verse the Jehovah's Witnesses changed?
>   *(a) John 1:1, The Word was with God, and the Word [Jesus] was God.*
>   *(b) John 1:1, The Word was with God and the Word [Jesus] was a god.*

You're correct if you chose (b). Of all the Greek scholars who have translated this passage not one translated it "a god." Reading it their way it means Jesus is NOT God and that is the way they want it. So who changed the Jehovah's Witnesses Bible? They did it themselves! See any red warning flags?

■ **Why would anyone choose not to go to heaven?**

The devil who rules this world has blinded the minds of those who do not believe. II Corinthians 4:4

The devil uses lies and deceit to blind your mind. So how do you become unblinded? Read God's word starting with the book of John.

■ **No one has ever seen God the Father, so how do we know what He is like?**

. . . Christ, who is exactly like God. II Corinthians 4:4

■ **Some trouble can become so devastating you might even think about giving up on life. You may be down but you are not defeated. Do not give up hope! Does God ever leave you?**

We have troubles all around us, but we are not defeated. We do not know what to do, but we do not give up the hope of living. We are persecuted, but God does not leave us. We are hurt sometimes, but we are not destroyed. II Corinthians 4:8, 9

■ **Will focusing on something else help to minimize current problems?**

We have small troubles for a while now, but they are helping us gain an eternal glory that is much greater than the troubles. We set our eyes not on what we see but on what we cannot see [heaven]. What we see will last only a short time, but what we cannot see will last forever. II Corinthians 4:17, 18

Try imagining what heaven will be like and see if that doesn't make your problems seem what they are—temporary.

■ **The older I become the more I contemplate the aging process. Does our spirit age along with us?**

Our physical body is becoming older and weaker, but our spirit inside us is made new every day. II Corinthians 4:16

Talking about what is inside us; what color is your soul? It's colorless to the eye because it is invisible. We interact with each other using our mind and that is part of the soul. So if you have racial prejudice, consider that the real person, the soul in each of us, is the same "color." Also, to God, is everyone the same?

Peter began to speak: "I really understand now that to God every person is the same." Acts 10:34

■ **Why did a Man who had no sin have to die for your sin?**

Christ had no sin, but God made him become sin so that in Christ we could become right with God. II Corinthians 5:21

You cannot be in God the Father's presence with unforgiven sin. The only thing that takes sin away is a blood sacrifice. The rest of the explanation can be said in two words—Good Friday.

■ **When is the right time to become right with God?**

I tell you that the "right time" is now, and the "day of salvation" is now. II Corinthians 6:2

Right now is the time! Pray this prayer. "Dear God, I want to live forever in heaven. I want to become a Christian. I confess to you I have sinned and I ask you to forgive me. I believe you sent your only son, Jesus Christ, to die on the Cross to pay for my sins. I believe He rose from the dead and lives today. I place my trust in You and I want to live for You from now on. Thank You for eternal life. Amen."[5]

■ How do you show someone you are a servant of God?

We show we are servants of God by our pure lives, our understanding, patience, and kindness, by the Holy Spirit, by true love, by speaking the truth, and by God's power. We use our right living to defend ourselves against everything. II Corinthians 6:6, 7

■ How can a poor person give to others and make them rich?

We are poor, but we are making many people rich in faith. We have nothing, but really we have everything. II Corinthians 6:10

■ Where does God dwell now since the Holy of Holies in the temple was destroyed in 70 AD?

The temple of God cannot have any agreement with idols, and we are the temple of the living God. II Corinthians 6:16

It's almost too much to fathom, but as a believer God lives in you.

■ What gift does the Holy Spirit have for you? Look up I Corinthians 12:4-10 to see what it is.

Did you look that up? Oh, your Bible wasn't handy so you were going to look it up later. I am just trying to get you into the habit of opening the most intriguing Book in the world, that's all.

Chapter Seven

"Believe me, sir, never a night goes by, be I ever so tired, but I read the Word of God before I go to bed."
- Douglas MacArthur -

■ **In heaven, will God be your Father?**

"I will be your father, and you will be my sons and daughters, says the Lord Almighty." II Corinthians 6:18

If you have a good earthly father that's great, but if you have a bad father I'm sorry. The happy ending is that all God's children get a wonderful, loving Father forever.

■ **What are your responsibilities as one who respects God?**

. . . so we should make ourselves pure—free from anything that makes body or soul unclean. We should try to become holy in the way we live, because we respect God. II Corinthians 7:1

■ **What does God want? Tune in when you see this short but profound question in the Bible.**

They first gave themselves to the Lord . . . . This is what God wants. II Corinthians 8:5

■ **When you hear a faith teacher say something like this, are you put on a guilt trip? "Give a gift of faith, like five hundred or a thousand dollars, and your faith will cause God to do a miracle in** your finances.   Plus, there will be a hundredfold return for yourself."

Give from what you have.   If you want to give, your gift will be accepted.   It will be judged by what you have, not by what you do not have. II Corinthians 8:11, 12

Don't be manipulated into giving what you don't have.

■ **The Old Testament law said to tithe. The word tithe literally means a tenth. What percent should the New Testament believer give?**

Each one should give as you have decided in your heart to give.   II Corinthians 9:7

Praise the Lord!   We are not under the law any longer as New Testament believers.   We are free to give more or less than 10%, but a tenth is still a good guideline.

■ **What should you keep in mind when you give to God?**

Remember this: The person who plants a little will have a small harvest, but the person who plants a lot will have a big harvest. II Corinthians 9:6

■ **True or false? If you feel forced to give or aren't pleased about doing it, you are probably better off just keeping the money.**

You should not be sad when you give, and you should not give because you feel forced to give. God loves the person who gives happily. II Corinthians 9:7

■ **Christians are talked about in the Holy Scriptures but are Jehovah's Witnesses and Mormons mentioned? Yes they are!**

So it does not surprise us if Satan's servants also make themselves look like servants who work for what is right. But in the end they will be punished for what they do. II Corinthians 11:15

OK, so not specifically mentioned by name, but all world religions and cults who don't confess Jesus is God are Satan's servants.

■ **Would an angel of light drag you unsuspectingly into hell for eternity? Guard yourself because the answer is dark—very dark!**

Even Satan changes himself to look like an angel of light. II Corinthians 11:14

This answer gives true light into the previous question as to how such nice people can deceive you into believing in their Jesus and not the Jesus of the Bible. If you don't know that Jesus is not "a god" as the Jehovah's Witnesses teach, you wouldn't know either that Satan has changed himself into an angel of light through those two "nice" people at your front door.

■ **Was Paul, the apostle, like an early day Billy Graham?**

I [Paul] had been in prison more often. I have been hurt more in beatings. I have been near death many times. Five times the Jews have given me their punishment of thirty-nine lashes with a whip. Three different times I was beaten with rods. One time I was almost stoned to death. Three times I was in ships that wrecked, and one of those times I spent a night and a day in the sea. II Corinthians 11:23-25

Paul was used by God to write a good portion of the New Testament and he was also an evangelist. But sometimes standing up for the truth and the real way of salvation is not always respected.

■ **Sometimes, is it for our own good that our problems and sicknesses are not taken away by God when we ask in prayer?**

I begged the Lord three times to take this problem away from me. But he said to me, "My grace is enough for you. When you are weak, my power is made perfect in you." II Corinthians 12:8, 9

■ **If almost everyone is driving five to ten miles an hour over the speed limit, is that confirmation that it's OK?**

We pray to God that you will not do anything wrong. It is not important to see that we have passed the test, but it is important that you do what is right . . . . II Corinthians 13:7

■ **Are you important to God? If He thought of** *you* **and made plans for** *you* **prior to** *your* **birth,** *you* **better believe** *you* **are important to God!**

But God had special plans for me and set me apart for his work even before I was born. Galatians 1:15

All the days planned for me were written in your book before I was one day old. Psalm 139:16

Do you have low self-esteem? Do you believe God inspired the Bible? If the answers were both yes, memorize the above and similar verses and then go and observe value in the mirror.

■ **Are there nice friendly people in your Bible study or church who do and say things that really don't seem to line up with what the Bible teaches?   It doesn't matter how prominent, wise or authoritative these people are, but what they do and say must agree with the Scriptures!   Are these people mistaken or are they deceivers?**

We talked about this problem because some false believers had come into our group secretly. They came in like spies to overturn the freedom we have in Christ Jesus. They wanted to make us slaves. But we did not give in to those false believers for a minute. We wanted the truth of the Good News to continue for you. Galatians 2:4, 5

■ **Do you have to do special things for God, say fervent prayers or follow strict rules to receive the Holy Spirit?**

Tell me this one thing: How did you receive the Holy Spirit? Did you receive the Spirit by following the law? No, you received the Spirit because you heard the Good News and believed it. You began your life in Christ by the Spirit. Galatians 3:2, 3

■ **Might God do miracles for you just for believing in His Son?**

Does God give you the Spirit and work miracles among you because you follow the law? No, he does these things because you heard the Good News and believed it. Galatians 3:5

■ **Can you be righteous in God's eyes if you obey the ten commandments?**

Now it is clear that no one can be made right with God by the law, because the Scriptures say, "Those who are right with God will live by trusting in him." Galatians 3:11

■ **Are you anti-Semitic?**

So you should know that the true children of Abraham are those who have faith. You belong to Christ, so you are Abraham's descendants. You will inherit all of God's blessings because of the promise God made to Abraham. Galatians 3:7, 29

If you have faith in Christ you are in the family of Abraham and he was the first Jew.

■ **Do you want to know what joy feels like? Contemplate the depths of what these words mean for you.**

Since you are God's children . . . . Galatians 4:6

■ **Why aren't all baby boys circumcised for religious purposes now?**

When we are in Christ Jesus, it is not important if we are circumcised or not. The important thing is faith—the kind of faith that works through love. Galatians 5:6

This ceremony was part of the Old Testament law but now we are living under God's grace and it becomes a choice.

■ **Do you have a relationship that needs healing—especially with your wife or husband? Can you do any better than advice from God?**

Serve each other with love. Galatians 5:13

■ **What will happen to a relationship if you don't serve each other with love?**

If you go on hurting each other and tearing each other apart, be careful, or you will completely destroy each other. Galatians 5:15

■ **If you don't obey God, do you obey the devil? Can you just be neutral?**

That same [evil] spirit is now working in those who refuse to obey God. Ephesians 2:2

You may think you can, but you can not be neutral.

"Whoever is not with me [Jesus] is against me. Whoever does not work with me is working against me. Matthew 12:30

■ **The devil is finally bound after the Tribulation period. Praise the Lord! But is he ever loosed again to tempt and harm people?**

When the thousand years are over, Satan will be set free from his prison. Then he will go out to trick the nations in all the earth . . . . Revelation 20:7, 8

You could call this the final trick or treat. Satan is set free for just a brief time before he is cast permanently into the lake of fire. God's purpose for this is to test the faith of only the people born during the Millennium.

■ **Which is the correct statement?**
    (1) Once we are born again we do good works because we are in favor with God.
    (2) We do good works so we can be in favor with God.

Salvation is not a reward for the good we have done, so none of us can take any credit for it. Ephesians 2:9 TLB

The correct answer is 1. No work for God will help in our salvation, but after salvation we will want to do good works because we are saved.

■ How is it possible to get near to God?

But now in Christ Jesus, you who were far away from God are brought near through the blood of Christ's death. Ephesians 2:13

Are you noticing that Jesus has done everything for us? Believer's sins are covered by His blood and that is the only way to get near to God.

■ God created the earth, but who named the third planet from the sun "earth?"

God named the dry land "earth" . . . . Genesis 1:10

■ This will be good news to some. Do you have to go through a minister, priest or religious leader to get to God?

. . . it is through Christ we all have the right to come to the Father .... Ephesians 2:18

The answer is no because we go directly to Christ in prayer. Through Him we have fellowship with God.

■ Where is God's country?

Now you are no longer strangers to God and foreigners to heaven, but you are members of God's very own family, citizens of God's country . . . . Ephesians 2:19 TLB

I joke that North Dakota and Minnesota are God's country, but in reality they are only heavenly. Get all excited though, because if you believe what Romans 10:9-10 says you are a citizen of God's country (heaven).

For if you tell others with your own mouth that Jesus Christ is your Lord, and believe in your own heart that God has raised him from the dead, you will be saved. For it is by believing in his heart that a man becomes right with God; and with his mouth he tells others of his faith, confirming his salvation. Romans 10:9-10 TLB

■ **Most people would say God created the world and of course that's true, but God is three persons in one. So between God the Father, Jesus, and the Holy Spirit, who did the actual creating?**

He [Jesus] is the One who created everything. Ephesians 3:9

■ **How much does God really love you?**

And I pray that you and all God's holy people will have the power to understand the greatness of Christ's love—how wide and how long and how high and how deep that love is. Christ's love is greater than anyone can ever know, but I pray that you will be able to know that love. Then you can be filled with the fullness of God. Ephesians 3;18, 19

Some people don't love themselves, so it's probably hard for them to understand how much God really loves and cares for them. This is my theological opinion: If you were to LET God show you how much He loves you, it wouldn't be long before you learned how to love yourself.

■ **If you <u>let</u> God work in your life, will good things start happening that you could never have imagined?**

With God's power working in us, God can do much, much more than anything we can ask or imagine. Ephesians 3:20

■ **Are you reading books trying to figure out how to have a successful marriage? Try the Good Book; it's full of advice that really works.**

Always be humble, gentle, and patient, accepting each other in love. Ephesians 4:2

■ **Should there be different denominations? There is only one God, one Bible, and one way to heaven—that's why I prefer a non-denominational Bible church. Denominations are OK but the higher question is, "Should there be different religions?"**

There is one body and one Spirit, and God called you to have one hope. There is one Lord, one faith, and one baptism. There is one God and Father of everything. Ephesians 4:4-6

There is only one religion that leads to heaven and it is Christianity.

■ **The body of Christ is the Church (people) and the head of the body is Jesus. How do you make the body of Christ stronger?**

And Christ gave gifts to people—he made some to be apostles, some to be prophets, some to go and tell the Good News, and some to have the work of caring for and teaching God's people. Christ gave those gifts to prepare God's holy people for the work of serving, to make the body of Christ stronger. This work must continue until we are all joined together in the same faith and in the same knowledge of the Son of God. Ephesians 4:11-13

Have you been called to tell people about Jesus? A few have been called to be preachers but all Christians, through the great commission, have been called to tell people about Jesus.

And He [Jesus] said to them, "Go into all the world and preach the gospel to every creature." Mark 16:15 NKJV

■ **Should one of your highest priorities be to become more like Christ?**

We must become like a mature person, growing until we become like Christ and have his perfection. Ephesians 4:13

■ **Are you a baby in Christ?**

We must become like a mature person, growing until we become like Christ and have his perfection. Then we will no longer be babies. We will not be tossed about like a ship that the waves carry one way and then another. We will not be influenced by every new teaching we hear from people who are trying to fool us. They make plans and try any kind of trick to fool people into following the wrong path. Ephesians 4:13, 14

Everyone starts as a baby in Christ, however, growth is a must for a Christian. Growth will protect you from misleading doctrines and false teachings. As you grow in truth, all this off-the-wall teaching will be very evident. For instance, how is it known that what the Mormon's teach can in no way get anyone to heaven? It is very simple when you grow in God's teachings. You learn Jesus is God from eternity past and the only way into heaven is through Jesus, who is deity, not Jesus who was a created man (Mormon belief). With knowledge of the truth it will be discovered that false religions put a twist on Christian terminology. They try to deceive, but now you have become smart and figured out they have their own hidden meanings to Bible words!

■ **How do people justify their behavior who steal, commit murder or live in immorality?**

They have lost all feeling of shame, and they use their lives for doing evil. Ephesians 4:19

■ **If something good can't be said about someone, should you keep your mouth shut? I figured we know each other by now so I can talk like a friend. I have a time in this area sometimes and figured you might too.**

When you talk, do not say harmful things, but say what people need— words that will help others become stronger. Then what you say will do good to those who listen to you. Ephesians 4:29

■ **Humans can not become angels. But to become an "angel" to people you know, how should you conduct yourself?**

Do not be bitter or angry or mad. Never shout angrily or say things to hurt others. Never do anything evil. Be kind and loving to each other, and forgive each other as God forgave you in Christ. Ephesians 4:31, 32

As can be seen, the book of Ephesians is full of good advice to live by. If you are a new Bible reader why don't you read the book of John first and then skip over and read Ephesians? It could be life changing!

■ **If you are "God's holy people" what important issues should you concentrate on avoiding?**

But there must be no sexual sin among you, or any kind of evil or greed. Those things are not right for God's holy people. Ephesians 5:3

■ **Is the Messiah the only person to be born who pre-existed himself?**

"But you, Bethlehem Ephrathah, though you are little among the thousands of Judah, yet out of you shall come forth to Me, the One [Jesus] to be ruler in Israel, whose goings forth have been from of old, from everlasting." Micah 5:2 NKJV

This verse is in the Old Testament telling of Jesus' birth! Reincarnation is a myth. No one has existed prior to their birth except Jesus, and He has been Jesus from eternity past. The Jews rejected Jesus as their Messiah, in part, because they were looking for a ruler to deliver them from the Romans, not from their sins. The Hebrew Scriptures in Daniel 9:26 (see below) told the Jews of Jesus' day that he would be cut off (killed). Do you suppose they didn't know this because they didn't read their Scriptures? Jesus is coming a second time and at that time He will rule and reign forever with His people.

■ **Is Bible prophecy fascinating, reliable and 100% accurate?**

After this period of 434 years, the Anointed One [the Messiah] will be killed, His kingdom still unrealized . . . and a king will arise whose armies will destroy the city [Jerusalem] and the Temple. Daniel 9:26 TLB

This passage from the Old Testament foretells that the Messiah would be killed prior to A.D. 70, the year Jerusalem and the temple were destroyed. If you are Jewish and looking for your Messiah He is in Daniel 9:26, Micah 5:2, Isaiah chapter 53, Psalm 22, and etc.

■ **Could the Bible have a subtitle of, "How To Have A Better Marriage?"**

Husbands, love your wives as Christ loved the church and gave himself for it. But each one of you must love his wife as he loves himself, and a wife must respect her husband. Ephesians 5:25, 33

■ God has promised us a long life full of blessing. What do you have to do to get it?

Children, obey your parents; this is the right thing to do because God has placed them in authority over you. Honor your father and mother. This is the first of God's ten commandments that ends with a promise. And this is the promise: that if you honor your father and mother, yours will be a long life, full of blessing. Ephesians 6:1-3 TLB

■ Dads, must you raise your children in the teaching of the Lord?

Fathers, do not make your children angry, but raise them with the training and teaching of the Lord. Ephesians 6:4

■ Do you want a new perspective of your work that will make it more meaningful and enjoyable?

In all the work you are doing, work the best you can. Work as if you were doing it for the Lord, not for people. Remember that you will receive your reward from the Lord, which he promised to his people. You are serving the Lord Christ. Colossians 3:23, 24

■ Is God going to treat you different from Billy Graham or Linda Kay Moskau (my wonderful Christian wife)?

Remember that the One who is your Master and their Master is in heaven, and he treats everyone alike. Ephesians 6:9

■ Is dying and being with Jesus going to be:
   a) Better than this life?
   b) As good as this life?
   c) Much better than you have it now?
   d) A drag because Jesus won't let you party?

I want to leave this life and be with Christ, which is much better. Philippians 1:23

Answer C is correct.

■ **If you were to die today, would it be a profit or a loss on your personal balance sheet?**

To me the only important thing about living is Christ, and dying would be profit for me. Philippians 1:21

It is profit to die and be in the presence of Jesus.

■ **Is God's Word full of humble advice to live by?**

. . . be humble and give more honor to others than to yourselves. Philippians 2:3

The main focus of this writing is to bring out interesting points of Scripture and answer many of life's questions. But there is so much good advice from your Creator of how you should live I just can't pass them up.

■ **This could be a "good news, bad news" scenario. Will everyone someday confess that Jesus is God?**

. . . so that every knee will bow to the name of Jesus—everyone in heaven, on earth, and under the earth. And everyone will confess that Jesus Christ is Lord . . . . Philippians 2:10, 11

I can't stress strongly enough to do it now while you are on the surface of the earth. Don't get caught dead doing it from under the surface of the earth.

■ **How big of a challenge can you take on?**

Do everything without complaining or arguing. Philippians 2:14

■ **True or false? Christians shine like stars in a dark world.**

But you are living with crooked and mean people all around you, among whom you shine like stars in the dark world. Philippians 2:15

Do other people know you shine? Metering your brightness can be a self-test to see where you are in your Christian growth.

■ **Are there commands that <u>don't</u> say, "Thou shalt not"?**

My brothers and sisters, be full of joy in the Lord. Philippians 3:1

■ **Is there anything greater than knowing Christ as Savior?**

. . . but I think that all things are worth nothing compared with the greatness of knowing Christ Jesus my Lord. Philippians 3:8

You won't really know what this means until you experience it.

■ **Is faith required to be made right with God?**

God uses my faith to make me right with him. Philippians 3:9

■ **Is heaven so great it will be like receiving a prize?**

I strain to reach the end of the race and receive the prize for which God is calling us up to heaven because of what Christ Jesus did for us. Philippians 3:14 TLB

■ **Jesus has a glorious resurrected body. Is your new glorified body going to be exactly like His?**

By his power to rule all things, he will change our simple bodies and make them like his own glorious body. Philippians 3:21

■ **Do you have a problem with God understanding why you have a physical or mental condition?**

God has made us what we are. In Christ Jesus, God made us to do good works, which God planned in advance for us to live our lives doing. Ephesians 2:10

Please allow me to be candid. God Himself made you the way you are for a purpose; now hop to it and start doing good things for God!

■ **If I were to tell you not to worry about anything, that would be counsel going in one ear and out the other. But if God told you not**

to worry, should that come in both ears and then settle deep in your soul?

Do not worry about anything, but pray and ask God for everything you need, always giving thanks. Philippians 4:6

■ **What do you think about?**

Brothers and sisters, think about the things that are good and worthy of praise. Think about the things that are true and honorable and right and pure and beautiful and respected. Philippians 4:8

Jim, I know you think about the Broncos occasionally, but for the rest of you how do your thoughts stack up against this list?

■ **Where does God get the things He gives you?**

My God will use his wonderful riches in Christ Jesus to give you everything you need. Philippians 4:19

Did that say want or need?

■ **If you are great, beautiful or handsome do you need to watch your pride extremely close?**

You became too proud because of your beauty. You ruined your wisdom because of your greatness. I threw you [Lucifer] down to the ground. Ezekiel 28:17

The first sin was pride. Lucifer (the devil) was thrown out of heaven because of it.

■ **Whoever paid for your sins can forgive your sins. Who alone has done that for you?**

The Son paid for our sins, and in him we have forgiveness. Colossians 1:14

Chapter Eight

"It is impossible to mentally or socially enslave
a Bible-reading people."
- Horace Greeley -

■ **Who is the god of this world?**

Satan, who is the god of this evil world . . . . II Corinthians 4:4 TLB

Was this a revelation to you? If it was you must protect yourself by filling your mind with God's truth, His Word.

■ **Because Satan is the god of this world, does that mean he is greater than God on earth?**

. . . because God's Spirit, who is in you, is greater than the devil, who is in the world. I John 4:4

■ **What word describes the devil's character and nature?**
   a) **Deceit**
   b) **Deceitful**
   c) **Deceiver**
   d) **Deceitfulness**

When he [Satan] tells a lie, he shows what he is really like, because he is a liar and the father of lies. John 8:44

Most people, Christians included, don't know their Bible well and can be deceived easily into believing something is Christian when, in reality

it is far from it.   Be ultra skeptical when you hear these words or concepts connected to "Christianity."

- *Where God is referred to as the: Transcendent, Higher Power, Inner Light or Source*
- *Spirit guide*
- *Spiritual practice*
- *Suggested reading includes books on spirituality*
- *God is explained as how your perceive him*
- *Holistic*
- *Mantra*
- *Yoga*
- *Centering*
- *Healing, where Jesus the Christ is not the healer*
- *The words prayer and meditation are used together along with other suspect concepts as listed here*

■ What is the devil's game?

He [the devil] was a murderer from the beginning and was against the truth, because there is no truth in him.   John 8:44

Let's put to practice what we just learned.   The god of this world (Satan) will tell you, "There are many paths to heaven.   Just being good is the requirement to get into heaven.   Everyone will see the light at the end of the tunnel when they die.   Being a member of the Catholic church will assure a place in heaven for you.   Jesus was just one of many good teachers."   Are you going to believe the god of this world, the father of lies, or the God of the Bible?

Don't get offended if you are Catholic.   I could have used Lutherans or any church or denomination.   The key point is membership means nothing, being born again means everything.

■ Is it possible to think and act like Jesus?

In your lives you must think and act like Christ Jesus.   Philippians 2:5

■ No one has even seen God the Father so how do we know what He is like?

No one can see God, but Jesus Christ is exactly like him. Colossians 1:15

■ **I've heard people say, "I've been a Christian all my life." Is that possible?**

At one time you were separated from God. You were his enemies in your minds, and the evil things you did were against God. Colossians 1:21

The answer is no and that is why you need to be born again.

■ **Wouldn't it be glorious at judgment day if God had nothing of which to accuse you guilty of?**

He [God] did this through Christ's death in the body so that he might bring you into God's presence as people who are holy, with no wrong, and with nothing of which God can judge you guilty. Colossians 1:22

■ **What is the only hope for glory? Who is the only hope for glory? What is the one hope you have for glory? What is your only chance for glory? I could go on you know but the point is there is only one ticket to heaven—don't throw it away.**

Christ . . . He is our only hope for glory. Colossians 1:27

As I write this section my wife and I are camping in beautiful Cedar City, Utah. The sad truth is that Mormons answer this question wrong. The major error of all cults is that they deny Jesus Christ of Nazareth is God. If you are in what Christianity calls a false religion, get a copy of a Bible that has been translated from manuscripts in the original languages. The New Century Version, the New American Standard Bible, New King James Version and others qualify. The truth is between those covers if you care to discover it. Anything outside the Bible is from the human mind.

■ **The arguments non-Christian religions have to justify their beliefs might seem good but are they?**

In him [Christ] all the treasure of wisdom and knowledge are safely kept. I say this so that no one can fool you by arguments that seem good, but are false. Colossians 2:3, 4

■ **I have heard that of all the people who go forward at a Billy Graham Crusade to receive Jesus, only 10% continue on in their new faith. I am sure the other 90% had good intentions but what did they fail to do?**

As you received Christ Jesus the Lord, so continue to live in him. Keep your roots deep in him and have your lives built on him. Be strong in the faith, just as you were taught, and always be thankful. Colossians 2:6, 7

■ **What tests in Scripture let people know if they are on track with God?**

Also, there must be no evil talk among you, and you must not speak foolishly or tell evil jokes. These things are not right for you. Instead, you should be giving thanks to God. You can be sure of this: No one will have a place in the kingdom of Christ and of God who sins sexually, or does evil things, or is greedy. Anyone who is greedy is serving a false god. Ephesians 5:4, 5

If you didn't score a high mark in each area may I suggest you hit "the Book."

■ **The teaching you receive from false religions comes from ruling spirits; so what's wrong with that?**

Be sure that no one leads you away with false and empty teaching that is only human, which comes from the ruling spirits of this world, and not from Christ. Colossians 2:8

These ruling spirits are the devil and his demons!

■ **Was Jesus 100% God and 100% man at the same time while He was on earth?**

All of God lives in Christ fully (even when Christ was on earth) . . . .
Colossians 2:9

■ Can you receive salvation by being baptized?

I mean that you have been saved by grace through believing. You did
not save yourselves; it was a gift from God. It was not the result of your
own efforts, so you cannot brag about it. Ephesians 2:8, 9

*The answer is no. Baptism is something you do (a work). God does not
permit any works to be counted toward salvation. It is totally a free gift
from God paid for by Jesus the Christ. If works were allowed, Jesus
could have saved Himself a trip to the Cross!*

■ Do you need to be baptized in order to enter heaven?

Jesus said to him [thief on the cross], "I tell you the truth, today you will
be with me in paradise." Luke 23:43

*You do not need to be baptized to enter heaven. However, baptism is
something you should do after being born again. Jesus told the thief
next to Him that because he believed he would be in paradise "today."
I am sure the Romans didn't take him down and allow a baptism. Also,
with Jesus telling him "today," explicitly says there is no waiting time
between death and being present with the Lord in heaven.*

We are confident, yes, well pleased rather to be absent from the body
and to be present with the Lord. II Corinthians 5:8 NKJV

■ Many people are baptized but what happens spiritually through it?

When you were baptized, you were buried with Christ, and you were
raised up with him through your faith in God's power that was shown
when he raised Christ from the dead. Colossians 2:12

*I don't want to argue this point with you but it did state, ". . . you were
raised up with him through your faith in God's power . . . ." Sorry, but
babies can not have faith in God—only people with reason can. I was
baptized as a baby, but when I found out it was something done as a*

voluntary decision after being born again, I was baptized again as a believer. Some of the things I bring up you may disagree with, and that's OK. But I pray I am prompting you to look into God's word and find out what it says. I don't want you to take my word for it either. Check it out yourself. Decide now to read through the Bible in a year or commit yourself to read the Scriptures five times a week. Acts 17:11 says to check out the Scriptures yourself to ensure what others teach you is correct.

■ **It is always right to follow examples set by Jesus. Was He baptized as a baby or a man?**

Then John said, "I saw the Spirit come down from heaven in the form of a dove and rest on him [at Jesus' baptism] ... But the God who sent me to baptize with water told me, 'You will see the Spirit come down and rest on a <u>man</u> [emphasis added] ....' "

■ **By what method did Jesus win the victory for your soul?**

With the cross, he won the victory . . . . Colossians 2:15

■ **Where is the only place to find truth and reality?**

But what is true and real has come and is found in Christ. Colossians 2:17

If you said the grocery store tabloids you need to come over and chat.

■ **Are you watching the evening news and taking it too seriously? Well, refresh your mind with this.**

Think only about the things in heaven, not the things on earth. Colossians 3:2

By the way, are you aware that the major newscasters are almost all liberal? You certainly are not getting unbiased news. I don't watch them too often but when I do I have my spiritual antenna up filtering out their liberal agenda.

■ **What happens to your old sinful self when you are born again?**

Your old sinful self has died, and your new life is kept with Christ in God. Colossians 3:3

■ What kind of things make God angry?

So put all evil things out of your life: sexual sinning, doing evil, letting evil thoughts control you, wanting things that are evil, and greed. This is really serving a false God. These things make God angry. Colossians 3:5, 6

God is kind, loving and very merciful. But when He says certain things make Him angry, perk up like you've never perked before?

■ Can a true Christian swear on a regular or semi-regular basis?

But now also put these things out of your life: . . . using evil words when you talk. Colossians 3:8

■ If you begin to live like a true Christian will you become like the One who created you?

You have begun to live the new life, in which you are being made new and are becoming like the One who made you. Colossians 3:10

■ What are the top three priorities in your life?

. . . Christ is all that is important. Colossians 3:11

If Christ was not number one, consider reevaluating your priorities. You will be pleasantly surprised at the results. The top three Biblical priorities are: God first, family second, and work third.

■ If you are a believer, the Holy Spirit resides in you. Does Jesus reside in the believer also?

But Christ is in all believers . . . . Colossians 3:11

■ The Scriptures state that God loves people, but does He get down to where the pizza sauce meets the dough and make it personal?

He loves you. Colossians 3:12

■ **If you can't get along with someone, would you be willing to try this command from God for help?**

Get along with each other, and forgive each other. Colossians 3:13

If someone does wrong to you, forgive that person because the Lord forgave you. Colossians 3:13b

Sorry, but not all these verses are going to give you warm, fuzzies. One of the toughest things to do is to forgive someone but you must do it.

■ **Christ holds the universe together but what holds life together?**

. . . but most important, love each other. Love is what holds you all together in perfect unity. Colossians 3:14

■ **We have been alerted to take notice when God says certain things make him angry, but what small statement on your part pleases God?**

And in all you do, give thanks to God the Father through Jesus. Colossians 3:17

■ **How should a person handle perplexing situations?**

Everything you do or say should be done to obey Jesus your Lord. Colossians 3:17

I like the statement for drugs, "Just say No." When I find myself debating how to deal with a situation I try to keep this saying in mind. "Just do what's right."

■ **Which of these two situations would you choose if you only had one choice?**
    1. Living in heaven where there is eternal joy with no pain, suffering, crying or death.
    2. Being in heaven sharing with Jesus all of God's treasures.

Remember that you will receive your reward from the Lord, which he promised to his people. Colossians 3:24

If Jesus is your Lord you don't have to choose because God is going to give you both. WOW!

■ **We pray for many different things, but have you prayed for this?**

Also pray for us that God will give us an opportunity to tell people his message. Colossians 4:3

Ask God for an opportunity and then it's as easy as lending someone a copy of this book.

■ **I am continually astonished when I overhear husbands and wives talking to each other. Often the talk is abrasive, sharp and blunt. Do you think the Holy Spirit has a suggestion for them?**

When you talk, you should always be kind and pleasant so you will be able to answer everyone in the way you should. Colossians 4:6

■ **What was the profession of Dr. Luke, who wrote the book of Luke?**

Demas and our dear friend Luke, the doctor, greet you. Colossians 4:14

Look, I'm trying to be as helpful as I can so you can answer many of these correctly. Remember to call the 800 number if you don't appreciate my ingenuous wit.

■ **Were some of the books in the New Testament originally written as letters?**

After this letter [book of Colossians] is read to you, be sure it is also read to the church in Laodicea. Colossians 4:16

■ **When a preacher puts on a show to present his message is he trying to impress God or the audience?**

But we speak the Good News because God tested us and trusted us to do it. When we speak, we are not trying to please people, but God, who tests our hearts. I Thessalonians 2:4

I have a hard time with preachers who put on a show when they minister God's word. Humor and good style are one thing but an act is something else.

■ **Talking about these showmen, do they often spend way too much time asking for money? One popular TV preacher I saw in person spent about 45 minutes just leading up to taking the offering, and that was before he put on his real show.**

We were not trying to get your money; we had no selfishness to hide from you. God knows that this is true. We were not looking for human praise, from you or anyone else, even though as apostles of Christ we could have used our authority over you. I Thessalonians 2:5-7

I have just given you two clues of wisdom when selecting TV and radio preachers. Don't get me wrong. I support Christian radio and TV, but use discernment. Use most of your discernment for television. There are only a few high profile TV preachers worth listening to! I don't want to come across as negative. I would like people to think I am wise, cautious and discriminating. So on a positive note these are preachers I think are worth listening to: Billy Graham, Hal Lindsey, Dr. D. James Kennedy, Zola Levitt, Dave Breese and Greg Laurie.

I can't stress strongly enough that you check out from a trustworthy source the people you listen to on radio and TV. If I didn't mention your favorites such as Kenneth Copeland, Robert Schuller, Oral Roberts, Kenneth Hagin or Benny Hinn, I highly suggest you research what these people and the people you listen to believe. For some of my research I use the Christian Research Institute, PO Box 7000, Rancho Santa Margarita, CA 92688-7000.

■ **It's nice to get a phone call from loved ones. Being called to supper is a pleasant beckoning too. Wouldn't the best call though be from your heavenly Father?**

. . . God, who calls you to his glorious kingdom. I Thessalonians 2:12

Ring. Ring. There's that call again. Do you want to answer it this time?

■ **Do you believe in a creation combo of God and evolution? Sounds like something on the menu board at a liberal seminary. Most people who believe this also believe there is a huge gap of time between the first two verses of Genesis.**

Evening passed, and morning came. This was the first day. Then God said, "Let there be something to divide the water in two." So God made the air and placed some of the water above the air and some below it. God named the air "sky." Evening passed, and morning came. This was the second day. Genesis 1:5-8

Sorry, but God is the only food for thought here—no combo. Two things will close that gap for you: (1) If there was a huge block of time between verses one and two there would have been a lot of dying going on. It states in I Corinthians 15:21 that death didn't come until after Adam sinned, and Adam wasn't created until after verse two! (2) If there was a large gap of time between those first two verses for evolution to take place, it was all done without the sun because it wasn't created until verse four. BAM! That noise was the gap slamming shut.

If I said the earth is 6,000 years old and you said it is 8,000 years old, there isn't that much to get concerned about. But if I said the earth is no older than 6-15,000 years and you said it was 4 1/2 billion years old, then one of us is definitely wrong. Time is the evolutionists friend—they say the earth is billions of years old, and generally creation scientists say it's only a few thousand years old. Given enough time, evolutionary theories may sound believable. But there is credible evidence that this old earth is actually quite young. If young is correct, is time really the evolutionists friend? Consider this scientific data for a young earth.

- *Helium escapes into the atmosphere but it is impossible for it to escape out of the atmosphere. At the rate of escape the atmosphere would be saturated with helium if the world were 4 1/2 billion years old. The actual rarity of that gas calculated out to reveal an estimated age of the earth at between 10 and 15,000 years old.*

- *At the rate space dust accumulates on the moon, the depth of it for 4 1/2 billion years should be 440 to 990 feet. The actual depth is only 1/8 to 3 inches! Using this measurement discloses an estimated earth age of 7 to 8,000 years old.*

- *A similar test of measuring meteoric dust on the earth discloses a young earth of 10 to 15,000 years old.*

- *From scientific measurements of the sun they know it is shrinking about five feet per hour. At this rate the sun would have had twice its present radius only 100,000 years ago. And only twenty million years ago the surface of the sun would have been touching the surface of the earth. This is very strong evidence that the entire universe is very young.*

- *One that is fairly technical is the scientific measurement of the earth's magnetic field. It is decaying by half every 1,400 years, so to back up just 10,000 years the strength of our magnetic field would equal that of the sun! Extrapolating these figures out indicates the earth's age to be 6 to 15,000 years old.[6]*

The book, "Origins Answer Book" by Paul S. Taylor on pages 18-20 list 102 similar illustrations that support evidence of earth being a young planet.

■ **Was creation completed in six days as we know days?**

He made the brighter light to rule the day and made the smaller light to rule the night . . . . Evening passed, and morning came. This was the fourth day. Genesis 1:16, 19

Yes, creation was six twenty-four hour days. The sun wasn't created until day four so couldn't the days before that have been real long? Sorry sunshine, but you don't need the sun to make a day. A day is one revolution of the earth! So pull the shades on the long days theory of creation please.

■ **Did you wonder what to wear today? Here is a suggestion from God of what to wear everyday.**

We should wear faith and love to protect us . . . . I Thessalonians 5:8

■ **If God the Father calls Jesus God, why do so many people have a problem believing that Jesus is God?**

But God said this about his Son [Jesus]: "God, your throne will last forever and ever." Hebrews 1:8

If the people who don't believe Jesus is God would read the infallible, inerrant, inspired Holy Scriptures with an open mind, the truth would fill their open-mindedness.

■ **The Jehovah's Witnesses believe Jesus is an angel! They can read these Scriptures just like you and I—are they deceived?**

This is because God never said to any of the angels, "You are my son. Today I have become your father." Nor did God say of any angel, "I will be his Father, and he will be my Son." And God never said this to an angel: "Sit by me at my right side until I put your enemies under your control." Hebrews 1:5, 13

Of course the Jehovah's Witnesses have a good sounding answer to cover over the truth of this Scripture. But who are you going to believe, God or something out of man's mind?

■ **Let's start a nationwide campaign to put this next verse on every bumper. The purpose? Eliminate annoying tailgaters.**

Be patient with everyone. I Thessalonians 5:14

■ **Should you trust everything your church believes? Should you test everything your minister, priest or spiritual leader tells you?**

But test everything. Keep what is good, and stay away from everything that is evil. I Thessalonians 5:21, 22

If I say you can gain heaven by attending a good church, being good or doing good for others, you better test that because it is wrong! The gravity of where a person spends eternity is so important. In fact it is the most important thing in your life! Determine right now to get yourself in a disciplined program of prayer and Bible reading. Your eternal health may depend on it. "But Mike," you say, "Take it easy, my church or pastor wouldn't deceive me." Maybe so, maybe not. How do you know they haven't been deceived? Don't trust your eternal life on what someone else says! Check it out against the Scriptures. How far will this argument get you? "But Satan, so-and-so told me if I was good and attended church I would go to heaven." The fire swallows you as Satan laughs and calls you a fool.

■ **Some books of the New Testament were written to specific churches or groups of people. How do we know they apply to us today?**

I tell you by the authority of the Lord to read this letter [I Thessalonians] to all the believers. I Thessalonians 5:27

We, today, are part of "all the believers."

■ **A synonym for God is love, so in the end will He punish someone for simply not believing in Jesus?**

Then he will punish those who do not know God and who do not obey the Good News about our Lord Jesus Christ. II Thessalonians 1:8

It is true God is love. He loves us so much He gave us a road map, the Bible, to find heaven. If you want to be stubborn and take another route then you have to suffer the consequences.

■ **If God is love, then how could He lovingly create Hell as a place for people to suffer in forever?**

Go into the fire that burns forever [hell] that was prepared for the devil and his angels. Matthew 25:41

God is love. Hell was prepared for Satan and his demons. God doesn't send anyone to hell. Your eternal soul was created with free will and so your destination is your choice. Hell has been enlarged to make room for people.

Therefore Sheol [hell] has enlarged itself and opened its mouth beyond measure .... Isaiah 5:14 NKJV

■ **Most accept that heaven is forever, but some put a time limit on those going to hell. Do people suffer in hell forever?**

Those people will be punished with a destruction that continues forever. II Thessalonians 1:9

"If heaven is better than we could dream of so hell will be worse than we can imagine." Quote from Greg Lauri, Bible teacher.

■ **Once in hell will a person's prayers be heard and will he have access to God?**

They [people in hell] will be kept away from the Lord and from his great power. II Thessalonians 1:9b

■ **I don't want to start any arguments, but it's a common belief that Adam committed the first sin. Is that correct?**

The woman saw that the tree was beautiful, that its fruit was good to eat, and that it would make her wise. So she took some of its fruit and ate it. She also gave some of the fruit to her husband, and he ate it. Genesis 3:6

■ **Does the Antichrist, that Man of Evil, claim he is God almighty?**

And that Man of Evil will even go into God's Temple and sit there and say that he is God. II Thessalonians 2:4

■ **Can you cite a Biblical incident where bad breath killed someone?**

Then that Man of Evil will appear, and the Lord Jesus will kill him with the breath that comes from his mouth and will destroy him with the glory of his coming. II Thessalonians 2:8

I used the term "bad breath" as a little levity but it may help in remembering the story.

■ **What one thing keeps most people from entering heaven?**

They will die, because they refused to love the truth. (If they loved the truth, they would be saved.) II Thessalonians 2:10

What is the truth? God's word, the Holy Bible, is truth.

■ **Who, after being made right with God, wrote one-third of the New Testament?**

Christ Jesus came into the world to save sinners, of whom I [Paul, the apostle] am the worst. But I was given mercy so that in me, the worst of all sinners, Christ Jesus could show that he has patience without limit. His patience with me made me an example for those who would believe in him and have life forever. I Timothy 1:15, 16

It was Paul who wrote nearly one third of the New Testament Scriptures. No matter how sinful or evil people become God can turn things around, forgive them, and use them mightily for the kingdom of God. Are you available to be used?

■ **What makes up the family of God?**

That family is the church of the living God, the support and foundation of the truth. I Timothy 3:15

Earlier we learned the Church is not any one organized church or building but it is all believers born from above.

■ **Channeling and spirit guides are popular today. Do these spirits tell you the truth of how to get to heaven?**

Now the Holy Spirit clearly says that in the latter time some people will stop believing the faith. They will follow spirits that lie and teachings of demons. I Timothy 4:1

If this is a revelation to you that spirit guides are really demons, you must set time aside to read the Scriptures. The truth will set you free and guide you to heaven!

■ **Vegetarians have a limited diet, but doesn't God tell us to feel free to eat everything He has provided?**

. . . foods which God created to be eaten with thanks . . . . Everything God made is good, and nothing should be refused if it is accepted with thanks. I Timothy 4:3-4

■ **Should you be very wary of Bible teachers or preachers who put an emphasis on saying God wants you to be wealthy?**

They [false teachers] think that serving God is a way to get rich. I Timothy 6:5

■ **Living in the world seems to get things all twisted up. Is the first step in becoming rich to be satisfied with what you have?**

Serving God does make us very rich if we are satisfied with what we have. I Timothy 6:6

The meaning of the word rich in the Scripture, is not speaking of monetary wealth but contentment.

■ **Is there anything wrong with wanting or having wealth?**

Those who want to become rich [monetary wealth] bring temptation to themselves and are caught in a trap. They want many foolish and harmful things that ruin and destroy people. I Timothy 6:9

If wanting wealth is your main goal in life please save yourself some misery.

■ **Can you imagine people throwing away eternal life for money?**

Some people have left the faith, because they wanted to get more money, but they have caused themselves much sorrow. I Timothy 6:10b

■ **Man says through his beer ads, "Grab all the gusto you can." What does God say to grab?**

Fight the good fight of faith, grabbing hold of the life that continues forever. I Timothy 6:12

■ **I've been declaring this all along and now here it is in black and white. What is the most important thing in your life?**

Some of these people have missed the most important thing in life— they don't know God. I Timothy 6:21 TLB

■ **Who is your hope for this life and the next?**

. . . and Christ Jesus our hope. I Timothy 1:1

. . . our Savior Christ Jesus. He destroyed death, and through the Good News he showed us the way to have life that cannot be destroyed. II Timothy 1:10

Shout glory! The One I have been telling you about has destroyed death!

■ **Is God's grace imparted to you at the same time as your salvation?**

That grace was given to us through Christ Jesus before time began . . . . II Timothy 1:9

■ **What types of things must you accomplish to earn your salvation?**

God, who . . . saved us and made us his holy people. That was not because of anything we did ourselves but because of God's purpose and grace. II Timothy 1:8-9

Nothing can be done to earn your salvation, it's a free gift. If there's one thing Christians should have is assurance of salvation (know now you would go directly to heaven when you die). In this verse, as in many others, it said God saved you. It didn't say you have to work out your own salvation nor that as you partake of the wafer and attend services you earn small fragments of "grace" and then someday you will be good enough to maybe enter heaven. No, you have salvation now and heaven is guaranteed for the Christian. My heart goes out to my Catholic friends who receive teachings that don't agree with the Word of God. No assurance of salvation or heaven in this statement by New York's

Cardinal O'Connor: "Church teaching is that I don't know, at any given moment, what my eternal future will be. I can hope, pray, do my very best—but I still don't know.   Pope John Paul II doesn't know absolutely that he will go to heaven, nor does Mother Teresa of Calcutta . . . ."[7]

You must read God's Word to find out the truth! Did you catch where Cardinal O'Connor made his error? He is depending on something out of the human mind, "Church teaching," rather than God's teaching— the Holy Scriptures.

■ **Is your church full of legalism and rules it has set up to show what you must do to please the church? It's time to unshackle and get rid of those chains.**

But God's teaching is not in chains. II Timothy 2:9

Follow God's Word, not man's traditions.

■ **Who would be so foolish as to reject glory that will never end?**

. . . [you] can have the salvation that is in Christ Jesus.   With that salvation comes glory that never ends. II Timothy 2:10

If telling others about Jesus is not easy for you, this might help. Choose someone you care about, but are unsure of their eternal destiny. Ask them, "How would you like to have glory that never ends?"   The conversation will go from there.

■ **Are you Jewish, Jehovah's Witness, Mormon, in a dead or liberal Catholic or Protestant church? Do you want to follow the true Jesus but are afraid of chastisement or criticism from your family or church? I wish I had an easy answer for you. However, eternal life is worth more than anything. If there is a persistent feeling to make a change—do it.**

His parents said this because they were afraid of the Jews, who had already decided that anyone who said Jesus was the Christ would be put out of the synagogue. John 9:22

I didn't write this book to make earthly friends; just eternal friends. The quote I am going to give you is going to make some so upset they will throw this book in the trash. Some peoples' trash is other peoples' treasure! The purpose of this shocking statement is to alarm you to the fact that what some churches teach is not enough to get you into heaven! They rely upon what has been substituted into church teaching rather than God's Holy Scriptures alone! If prominent, knowledgeable, theologically sound Bible based Christian leaders were saying this about my church I would naturally get upset, but then I would be checking this out like my eternal life depended on it! Hank Hanegraaff, President of Christian research Institute said on his radio program the "Bible Answer Man" on December 31, 1997, "It's the exception rather than the rule that a Catholic is saved." Mr. Hanegraaff loves Catholics, but he has wisely discerned that the teachings of the Catholic Church have almost entirely moved away from the saving faith in Jesus alone.

■ **This book is basically about finding out what the truth is from the source of truth, the Holy Spirit. The only source of truth says in Genesis 1:27, "So God created human beings in his image." With this truth you are now so wise that even if the pope said, "Fresh knowledge leads to recognition of the theory of evolution as more than just a hypothesis," you would know instantly that the pope is off his dinosaur. The supporting Scripture below refers to rising from the dead, but the principle of leaving the truth is what we are looking at.**

They have left the true teaching saying that the rising from the dead has already taken place and so they are destroying the faith of some people. II Timothy 2:18

When you run into a difficult situation ask yourself, "What does common sense tell me?" Do you believe just a man (Darwin) who came up with just a theory. And in that theory he admitted the weak link was that no transitional forms had been found, or do you believe God who is the source of all truth? If there are no transitional forms, where do the pictures in our kids' school books come from? They are from the artist's mind because there is absolutely no physical evidence for these drawings!

More and more well known evolutionists are finally facing the truth to the question of, "Where's the beef"(proof of evolution)? Evolutionist Edmund Ambrose stated, "We have to admit that there is nothing in the geological records that runs contrary to the view of conservative creationists . . . ."[8] Isaac Asimov, prolific science writer, stated, "I don't have the evidence that God doesn't exist."

■ **How do you get wisdom and become wise? Watching TV talk shows is not the correct answer.**

. . . the Holy Scriptures which are able to make you wise. II Timothy 3:15

If you are not wise you are ignorant, simple, foolish and dull. You can get upset with me for saying that if you want, but if it plants a seed for you to read the Scriptures, I'll take the abuse.

■ **So what purpose or good is wisdom?**

And that wisdom leads to salvation through faith in Christ Jesus. II Timothy 3:15b

Does life get any better than this? Yes. As you begin to read your Bible, starting at the book of John, you will receive wisdom that leads to eternal life.

John F. Kennedy was smart enough, but was he wise enough to choose eternal life? Judith Campbell Exner was an intimate friend of the married President. Recently she made this statement about his dark side. "He was so bright, I just wish he had been wiser."

■ **As a believer do you have a responsibility to tell others how to get to heaven? You might say, "I don't know the Bible well enough to tell others," or "I'm too shy," or "Don't rock the boat, just let people believe what they believe," or "I'm sure most people are going to heaven so why do I have to get out of my comfort zone?"**

Jesus said to his followers, "Go everywhere in the world, and tell the Good News to everyone." Mark 16;15

Sorry if this made you feel uneasy. I did some research after reading in Matthew 7:13-14 that only a few people are going to make it to heaven. This research revealed that "few" translates to about 5% of the world's population. Compare your comfort zone to someone spending eternity in hell. The research can be found in a booklet I wrote and information about it is under "Suggested Reading" at the end of this book.

■ **Other than the message of salvation what are some major reasons why the Bible was written?**

. . . to help the faith of God's chosen people and to help them know the truth that shows people how to serve God. Titus 1:1

Have you noticed how many times the word truth has been mentioned? God knew there would be much deception so He preserved the truth for YOU in His book, the Bible.

■ **Could God lie if He wanted to?**

And God cannot lie. Titus 1:2

■ **By survey over 80% of people say they believe in God, but on the other hand the Scriptures tell us there are only a few people who really know God in a saving way. How can we tell which ones are the real Christians?**

They say they know God, but their actions show they do not accept him. Titus 1:16

If a person goes to church on Sunday morning and then lives like the rest of the world (no thought or care about God) during the week, are they part of the over 80% or part of the few?

■ **Do you deserve to be treated as if you are somebody important?**

Do not let anyone treat you as if you were unimportant. Titus 2:15

■ **If God wrote you a letter expressing how He would like you to live; what would He tell you?**

Remind the believers to yield to the authority of rulers and government leaders, to obey them, to be ready to do good, to speak no evil about anyone, to live in peace, and to be gentle and polite to all people. Titus 3:1-2

This letter (book of Titus) from God was written by Paul to Titus and all believers.

■   **This issue of works, doing something on your part to earn salvation, is so important I thought I would address it from yet another book of the Bible. What specific deeds or works must you do to earn your way into heaven?**

But when the kindness and love of God our Savior was shown, he saved us because of his mercy. It was not because of good deeds we did to be right with him. Titus 3:4, 5

Salvation is plain and simple to those who believe and ask. It's a free gift from God—no works attached.

I was going to end my comment, but what some people have been taught makes my righteous indignation red hot. Did this verse say ANYTHING about the requirement to belong to a certain church to be saved? Did it say ANYTHING about a mandate to attend services religiously? If your church teaches these things it is incorrect. Going to church is very important for growth and fellowship but not required to be a Christian. The Bible is your personal eternal life insurance policy. Read it like your eternal destiny depends on it.

■ **Paul, who wrote more of the New Testament than anyone, wrote some of it while he was in prison. Why was he in jail?**

... I am in these chains for preaching the Good News . . . .   Philemon 1:13 TLB

■   **Even with the help of Jesus is it possible for you to attain holiness?**

Jesus, who makes people holy . . . . Hebrews 2:11

■ **Who is the High Priest of your faith?**

. . . Jesus, who was sent to us and is the high priest of our faith. Hebrews 3:1

■ **What brand of genes must you have in order to be a Jewish priest?**

The people were given the law based on a system of priests from the tribe of Levi . . . . Hebrews 7:11

■ **While Jesus was a man on earth for 33 years did He ever sin?**

Jesus . . . He is holy, sinless, pure, not influenced by sinners, and he is raised above the heavens. Hebrews 7:26

■ **Is there life in the universe other than the people of earth?**

Christ offered his sacrifice only once and for all time when he offered himself. But after Christ offered one sacrifice for sins, forever, he sat down at the right side of God. Hebrews 7:27, 10:12

If we accept the Bible as true, then we believe God offers salvation to living souls. He did that through Christ, once for all time, and He did that on earth. If other intelligent life exists somewhere else there is no means of salvation for them and God would not allow that.

I believe in UFOs but I also believe they are manifestations from the evil spirit world. What is the purpose of UFOs then? We have learned that the devil's best trick is deception. At the end of the present age when God takes the living believers to heaven in the Rapture the people left on earth will have to explain what happened. I believe there will be an increase in UFO sightings and activity as we draw closer to this catching away. When this great event, the Rapture, happens deceived people will say the earth has been purged of Christians and they were removed by aliens in UFOs!

■ **There have been fictional movies made about the Ark of the Covenant that was in the old Jewish Temple. It's possible that the**

Ark will be discovered soon and if it's the real thing what should be inside of it?

Inside the ark were the tablets of stone with the Ten Commandments written on them, and a golden jar with some manna in it, and Aaron's wooden cane that budded. Hebrews 9:4 TLB

■ Blessings from God are highly prized but how long do they last?

Those who are called by God can now receive the blessings he has promised, blessings that will last forever. Hebrews 9:15

■ Who do you call when you need help?

He [Jesus] went into heaven itself and is there now before God to help us. Hebrews 9:24

The person who created you is ready, willing, and able to help you now, just call on Him.

■ Can it be said that something alive is not real? Of course not.

God's word is alive and working and is sharper than a double-edged sword. It cuts all the way into us, where the soul and the spirit are joined . . . . Hebrews 4:12

■ Would it surprise you if the best explanation of what faith is comes right from the Word of God?

Faith means being sure of the things we hope for and knowing that something is real even if we do not see it. Hebrews 11:1

■ What must you have to please God?

Without faith no one can please God. Hebrews 11:6

■ How do you know that you know that God created the world?

It is by faith we understand that the whole world was made by God's command so what we see was made by something that cannot be seen. Hebrews 11:3

Chapter Nine

"I have for many years made it a practice to read
through the Bible once a year."
- John Quincy Adams -

■ **God's reward for you is better than all the treasures of Egypt!**
Are you going for it?

He [Moses] thought it was better to suffer for the Christ than to have all
the treasures of Egypt, because he was looking for God's reward.
Hebrews 11:26

God's reward of eternal life and all that goes with it is worth more than
anything.

■ **Some of the hardships we go through are just pure discipline**
from our loving heavenly Father. So why would God discipline
sweet, hard-hearted individuals?

But God disciplines us to help us, so we can become holy as he is.
Hebrews 12:10

■ **If you live a decent wholesome life, but not a holy life, can you**
still make it to heaven?

Anyone whose life is not holy will never see the Lord. Hebrews 12:14

Your responsibility in life is to believe on God's Son and then try and
live like Jesus lived.

■ Movies, TV and possibly some of your "friends" are telling you it's the 90s so don't be a prude. What is a righteous God telling you?

God will judge as guilty those who take part in sexual sins. Hebrews 13:4

The average person watches four hours of TV a day. Would your views on morality change if you substituted one hour of Bible reading for one hour of Jerry Springer, Jenny Jones or Ricki Lake?

■ God will come near to you if you:
    a. work your fingers to the bone for Him
    b. attend church religiously
    c. give at least 10% of your income to Him
    d. come near to Him

Come near to God, and God will come near to you. James 4:8

■ Surely with all the beautiful well-protected cities of the world some should survive and go on forever. Shouldn't they?

Here on earth we do not have a city that lasts forever, but we are looking for the city that we will have in the future [the new Jerusalem]. Hebrews 13:14

At the end of the Millennium the earth and all its cities are burned up, but it is replaced by a beautiful new earth.

■ Is there a good spiritual purpose in the troubles you have.

My brothers and sisters, when you have many kinds of troubles, you should be full of joy, because you know that these troubles test your faith, and this will give you patience. James 1:2-3

■ If sin is allowed to grow what will it produce?

. . . and then the sin grows and brings death. James 1:15

■ What is a prime reason for not becoming angry easily?

Do not become angry easily, because anger will not help you live the right kind of life God wants. James 1:19-20

■ **I hear people talk about their religion and later out of the same mouth I hear foul four letter words, the Lord's name taken in vain or off-color stories. What does that tell of their religion?**

People who think they are religious but say things they should not say are just fooling themselves. Their "religion" is worth nothing. James 1:26

So then, rid yourselves of all evil, all lying, hypocrisy, jealousy, and evil speech. I Peter 2:1

■ **In God's way of thinking is this statement true? It is not a sin to think that some people are more important than others.**

My dear brothers and sisters, as believers in our glorious Lord Jesus Christ, never think some people are more important than others. But if you treat one person as being more important than another, you are sinning. James 2:1, 9

■ **Who will be judged more strictly—the Bible teacher or the believer who hears the teaching?**

. . . we who teach will be judged more strictly. James 3:1

■ **What part of your body is: wild and evil, full of deadly poison, spreads evil throughout your entire body, set on fire by hell and cannot be tamed?**

And the tongue is like a fire. It is a whole world of evil among the parts of our bodies. The tongue spreads its evil through the whole body. The tongue is set on fire by hell . . . no one can tame the tongue. It is wild and evil and full of deadly poison. James 3:6, 8

■ **Where you find jealousy and selfishness you will also find _____ and _____.**

Where jealousy and selfishness are, there will be confusion and every kind of evil. James 3:16

■ **If you knew the root cause of your fights and arguments wouldn't that give you a starting point to work with?**

Do you know where your fights and arguments come from? They come from the selfish desires that war within you. James 4:1

If this is an area that needs attention in your life consider that the Scripture just pointed out the problem.

■ **Is this a true statement? Loving the world is hating God.**

You should know that loving the world is the same as hating God. James 4:4

Loving the world means loving its evil pleasures. Might that include most movies? How many of them would you take Jesus along to see?

■ **If you stand against the devil he will:**
    a. **crush you**
    b. **really get on your case**
    c. **run from you**
    d. **trip you up**
    e. **all the above**
    f. **none of the above**

Stand against the devil, and the devil will run from you. James 4:7

The correct answer is c.

■ **If you know the right thing to do but don't do it, is that a sin?**

Anyone who knows the right thing to do, but does not do it, is sinning. James 4:17

■ **We seem to think we have to give reasons and long winded excuses when we answer somebody. What's wrong with yes or no and a period?**

Don't use the name of heaven, earth, or anything else to prove what you say. When you mean yes, say only yes, and when you mean no, say only no so you will not be judged guilty. James 5:12

■ What's the first thing you should do when trouble shows up?

Anyone who is having troubles should pray. James 5:13

■ Do you need to be healed of a serious ailment?

Anyone who is sick should call the church's elders. They should pray for and pour oil on the person in the name of the Lord. And the prayer that is said with faith will make the sick person well; the Lord will heal that person . . . . Confess your sins to each other and pray for each other so God can heal you. James 5:14-16

Nothing is too difficult for the Lord. God is love and God is good but God is also sovereign which means He decides who is healed, for what purpose, and when.

■ What happens when a believing person prays?

When a believing person prays, great things happen. James 5:16b

■ What is unique about Jesus compared to gods of other religions?

. . . because Jesus Christ rose from the dead. I Peter 1:3

Jesus, who rose from the dead, will also raise all believers. It follows then that gods of other religions who have not been able to raise themselves will not raise anyone else either. All religions are dead except Christianity!

■ What commodity is so precious it can buy human souls?

You were bought, not with something that ruins like gold or silver, but with the precious blood of Christ . . . . I Peter 1:18-19

■ Will becoming a true Christian have an effect on your lifestyle?

Now that you are obedient children of God do not live as you did in the past. I Peter 1:14

Yes, your life will be changed—for the better.

■ **Can you be a Christian but yet have problems with lust, adulterous thoughts, alcohol, drugs, and etc.?**

I beg you to avoid the evil things your bodies want to do that fight against your soul. I Peter 2:11

Yes, Christians battle some of these sins even after they decide to follow Jesus.

■ **If you live like a servant will it please God, slay your enemies and astound your friends?**

Live as servants of God. Show respect for all people: Love the brothers and sisters of God's family, respect God, honor the king. I Peter 2:16, 17

■ **I feel for married couples where only one is a believer and they desire more than anything that the other become a believer. They try hard to win them over by all kinds of innovative ways. Is a tract on the coffee table innovative? It's a good try anyway. What is a frustrated spouse to do?**

Then, if some husbands do not obey God's teaching, they will be persuaded to believe without anyone's saying a word to them. They will be persuaded by the way their wives [and husbands] live. I Peter 3:1

■ **How do you keep foolish people from saying stupid things about you?**

It is God's desire that by doing good you should stop foolish people from saying stupid things about you. I Peter 2:15

■ **What is the difference between a real and a false prophet?**

No prophecy in the Scriptures ever comes from the prophet's own interpretation. No prophecy ever came from what a person wanted to say, but people led by the Holy Spirit spoke words from God. II Peter 1:20, 21

The difference is a real prophet gets his information from the Holy Spirit and is precisely correct all the time. A false prophet thinks up his own predictions of coming events and is nearly always wrong. An excellent way to tell the Scriptures are true is predictive prophecy. The Bible is the <u>only</u> holy book that tells of events before they happen. Of the prophecies that have come to pass, 100% of them have been precisely accurate. Compare that to the prognosticators of future events in grocery store tabloids where they are extremely lucky if they hit 1 out of 10 predictions.

■ **With God all things are possible, so can this be a true statement? A facially deficient person can actually be beautiful.**

It is not fancy hair, gold jewelry, or fine clothes that should make you beautiful. No, your beauty should come from within you—the beauty of a gentle and quiet spirit that will never be destroyed and is very precious to God. I Peter 3:3, 4

■ **As a Christian how does God see you?**

But you are a chosen people, royal priests, a holy nation, a people for God's own possession. I Peter 2:9

■ **We mistakenly think we choose God, but it was actually God who chose us. Why were you chosen?**

You were chosen to tell about the wonderful acts of God, who called you out of darkness into his wonderful light. I Peter 2:9b

God chooses everyone, but only a few accept what He has to offer.

■ **Other than for your own salvation why do you need to study and learn God's word?**

Always be ready to answer everyone who asks you to explain about the hope you have . . . . I Peter 3:15

People who don't know that Christianity is the only way to heaven are going to ask you basic questions like these. How can you know the Bible is true, accurate or inspired? How can the man Jesus be God? Isn't it narrow minded to say only Christians go to heaven? Can you tell me precisely how I get to heaven? The way to "always be ready to answer" is to know your Bible well.

■ **Some people believe that at death your spirit goes into an unconscious state called soul sleep until the resurrection.   The Scriptures state we will be like Christ. Did His spirit sleep after He was killed?**

His body was killed but he was made alive in the spirit and in the spirit he went and preached to the spirits in prison. I Peter 3:18 19

We are confident, yes, well pleased rather to be absent from the body and to be present with the Lord. II Corinthians 5:8 NKJV

■ **Is being hospitable part of being a Christian?**

Open your homes to each other, without complaining. I Peter 4:9

I like that verse. Looks like we provide the airfare and you provide the housing. We have never been to Hawaii or a cabin on a Minnesota lake would be nice also. This sounds a little bold coming from me, but I just want to obey the Scriptures. Please mail invitations to PO Box 5172, Golden, CO 80401. See you soon!

■ **As people we don't want trouble, but as Christians we should get used to the idea that it is going to come our way. Why should we assume serious trouble is going to seek us out?**

Dear friends, don't be bewildered or surprised when you go through the fiery trials ahead, for this is no strange, unusual thing that is going to happen to you. Instead, be really glad—because these trials will make you partners with Christ in his suffering, and afterwards you will have the wonderful joy of sharing his glory in that coming day when it will be displayed. I Peter 4:12, 13 TLB

■ **What happens when people insult you because of your love for Jesus?**

When people insult you because you follow Christ, you are blessed, because the glorious Spirit, the Spirit of God, is with you. I Peter 4:14

■ **If you don't believe the Bible teaches that Jesus is God, does that mean your only alternative is to believe something that is not true?**

. . . our God and Savior Jesus Christ . . . . II Peter 1:1

It's distressing that so many people don't accept the truth that Jesus is God the Savior. Consider that over thousands of years no one has been able to prove the Scriptures are wrong.

■ **Does everyone have the ability to serve God?**

Jesus has the power of God, by which he has given us everything we need to live and to serve God. II Peter 1:3

■ **How serious is it to believe what a false teacher/preacher says? Is it so serious that you could end up in hell forever because of what they say?**

There used to be false prophets among God's people, just as you will have some false teachers in your group. They will secretly teach things that are wrong—teachings that will cause people to be lost [end up in hell]. They will even refuse to accept the Master, Jesus, who bought their freedom. II Peter 2:1

■ **Are there many or few people believing false preachers today?**

Many [emphasis added] will follow their evil ways and say evil things about the way of truth. II Peter 2:2

Have you checked out who you listen to? You may be in a mainline denomination and feel secure, but if it or the pastor is liberal in beliefs, their teachings could send people in the opposite direction of heaven. Some of these points get hard or personal but we are talking heaven, hell, and eternity. Most people believe they are going to heaven but the Bible says just a few are! So how do you tell if what you are being taught is following the straight and narrow path that leads to eternal life?

> *1. A person or church must believe these essentials of the historic Christian church.*
>> *a. The Bible is without error.*
>> *b. Jesus is God from eternity past.*
>> *c. Jesus was born of a virgin.*
>> *d. We are saved by the shed blood of Jesus alone.*
>> *e. Jesus rose from the dead.*

When inquiring about a church, organization or individual don't take any roundabout answers. They must either believe or disbelieve each fundamental point. You can get these answers by asking for a printed statement of beliefs.

> *2. The Christian Research Institute (CRI) does an excellent job in digging out the truth of who believes what. They can give you specific answers on individuals, denominations, and churches. Write them at: PO Box 7000, Rancho Santa Margarita, CA 92688-7000.*
>
> *3. If you don't know for certain, please don't assume your teacher/preacher or denomination is OK. Remember II Peter 2:2 said MANY are following false beliefs.*

I wrote to CRI about a concern I had with a denomination that has merged several of its branches. With mergers come compromise—some good, some bad. I am familiar with this denomination and what I confirmed is going to shock some of you. Others could get upset, but maybe a few will be thankful for the insightful truth brought to light. This is the statement I received from them.

> *"The Association of Evangelical Lutherans (AEL), the American Lutheran Church (ALC), and the Lutheran Church in America (LCA) have merged into what is now called the Evangelical Lutheran Churches of America (ELCA). This merged body does not officially hold to the inerrancy of the Bible, yet they believe it to be "inspired"; that is, they say the Scriptures can be inspired while at the same time contain error in historical, geographical and scientific statements. For this reason, we do not recommend this branch of Lutheranism. The most conservative of the major*

branches of Lutheranism is the Lutheran Church—Missouri Synod (LC-MS); this branch does hold to the inerrancy of the Bible. We do, therefore, recommend the LC-MS as an orthodox denomination."
Where essentials of the historic Christian church are in question, get all the counsel you can. David Hocking, a national expositional Bible teacher, says his first criteria of a good church to join is one that believes in the inerrancy of the Bible! Falling away from one essential is way too many but the ELCA seminary professors are even pulling back from the fundamental belief that Jesus was born of a virgin! See 1c listed above. Another good source of solid information on the faultering beliefs of the ELCA is: Christian News, 3277 Boeuf Lutheran Road, New Haven, MO 63068-2213. Phone: (573)237-3110.

■ **Sodom and Gomorrah were two cities full of sexual sin, including men with men and women with women. Why did God destroy those towns, Ellen?**

And God also destroyed the evil cities of Sodom and Gomorrah by burning them until they were ashes. He made those cities an example of what will happen to those who are against God. II Peter 2:6

■ **After the Great Tribulation period, will the nature of animals be different?**

Then wolves will live in peace with lambs, and leopards will lie down to rest with goats. Calves, lions, and young bulls will eat together, and a little child will lead them. Isaiah 11:6

■ **What question can you pose to someone to find out if they are on God's side or with the enemy (the devil)?**

My dear friends, many false prophets have gone out into the world. So do not believe every spirit, but test the spirits to see if they are from God. This is how you can know God's Spirit: Every spirit who confesses that Jesus Christ came to earth as a human is from God. And every spirit who refuses to say this about Jesus is not from God. I John 4:1-3

The question you should ask is: Do you believe Jesus Christ came to earth as a human?

■ **Do you have to love God in order to know him?**

Whoever does not love does not know God, because God is love. I John 4:8

■ **What is the test to find out who is a child of God?**

If you believe that Jesus is the Christ—that he is God's Son and your Savior—then you are a child of God. I John 5:1 TLB

Read that verse carefully because many believe the first two criteria, but only a few have made Jesus Savior through a personal relationship. A personal relationship develops as you get to know Him through hearing and reading God's Word.

■ **I believe in not trashing the planet we live on and controlling businesses and people from polluting. But is it possible to substitute the environmental cause for the truth of God?**

They traded the truth of God for a lie. They worshipped and served what had been created instead of the God who created those things, who should be praised forever. Amen. Romans 1:25

■ **Can someone miss heaven because they didn't understand the Bible or God?**

We also know that the Son of God has come and has given us understanding so that we can know the True One. I John 5:20

■ **What is one way to stay safe no matter what happens?**

To all who have been called by God. God the Father loves you, and you have been kept safe in Jesus Christ: Jude 1

Like the motto says, "Safety Pays." Just don't try and bring this up at your monthly safety meeting at work or you will find out what persecution means.

■ **Jim Jones and David Koresh—what did they have in common? Power? Money? Yes. Yes. They also were both having sex with their followers. Is sex a major reason why these cult leaders use religion as a cover-up for their perversion?**

Long ago the prophets wrote about these people who will be judged guilty. They are against God and have changed the grace of our God into a reason for sexual sin. They also refuse to accept Jesus Christ, our only Master and Lord. Jude 4

■ **Are all bad angels (demons) free to make life miserable for people or are some so bad they have been destined to chain smoke until they meet the Judge?**

And remember the angels who did not keep their place of power but left their proper home [heaven]. The Lord has kept these angels in darkness [hell], bound with everlasting chains, to be judged on the great day. Jude 6

■ **Is there ever "forever" going to be a nice sunny bright day in hell?**

A place in the blackest darkness has been kept for them forever. Jude 13

This verse also shows, through the term "blackest," that there are different degrees of punishment for the inhabitants of the place of the damned.

■ **Do you think about what heaven is going to look like? Does God have a garden in paradise?**

"To those who win the victory I will give the right to eat the fruit from the tree of life, which is in the garden of God." Revelation 2:7

The garden of Eden was probably patterned after the garden in heaven.

■ **Does it do any good to hide or run from God when He knows where you live?**

"The One [God] who has the sharp, doubled-edged sword says this: I know where you live." Revelation 2:12, 13

■ **God is our Heavenly Father, so isn't it logical that a father would name his children?**

"I will also give to each one who wins the victory a white stone with a new name written on it." Revelation 2:17

You will receive your new name in heaven.

■ **What color are clothes going to be in heaven?**

". . . so they will walk with me [Jesus] and will wear white clothes, because they are worthy." Revelation 3:4

White stands for purity, righteousness, and goodness. You are worthy solely because you are made righteous before God through Jesus. It's not because of your own efforts.

■ **A hot controversy exists about this topic: "Once saved, always saved." The longer I study this the more I am convinced a person can't lose their salvation. I like these two thoughts from Chuck Missler. In the natural you were born, but can you make yourself unborn? The obvious answer is no. To carry that over to the spiritual side, if you were born again can you make yourself unborn? I don't think so. And consider the ark of Noah as a type of salvation. The eight people inside were saved. The door on the ark was so heavy God had to close it and shut them in. Could these saved people have opened the door and gotten out of the ark? I don't think so. So what do you think? Is there an eraser on God's pen that was used to put your name in the book of life?**

"And I will not erase their names from the book of life, but I will say they belong to me before my Father and before his angels. This is what the One who is holy and true . . . says. When he opens a door, no one can close it. And when he closes it, no one can open it." Revelation 3:5, 7

■ **What is the purpose of the seven year Tribulation period?**

"So I will keep you from the time of trouble that will come to the whole world to test those who live on earth." Revelation 3:10

Note that in the verse God promises Christians He will keep them from this trouble. You might be questioning that if God is good and loving, why does He make anyone go through this time of testing? God is love and God is good; it's humans with a sin nature that is the problem!

■ What is an important purpose for the Millennium?

"Listen! I am coming soon! I will bring my reward with me, and I will repay each one of you for what you have done." Revelation 22:12

It's a time of reward for the children of God.

■ How can you have wealth yet be called poor by God?

"You say, 'I am rich, and I have become wealthy and do not need anything.' But you do not know that you are really miserable, pitiful, poor, blind, and naked." Revelation 3:17

The context of the verse is that wealthy people had it all except for eternal life. At this writing we are at Marble, Colorado, one of the most beautiful spots on earth, especially in the fall when the aspen leaves are gold. The campground manager alluded to the area as paradise. I agreed, and then thought we can only enjoy this paradise for several days now. But as people who know Jesus as Savior and Lord, someday we will be able to spend all our time in true paradise. I not only had a nice day, but that exciting thought made my day.

■ Why do bad things happen to good Christians?

"I correct and punish those whom I love. So be eager to do right, and change your hearts and lives." Revelation 3:19

Just like parents want to keep their kids on the straight and narrow, God does too. He uses correction and punishment to keep you from straying too far.

■ Are your prayers like a sweet smell to God?

. . . golden bowls full of incense, which are the prayers of God's holy people. Revelation 5:8

This reminds me of a story from the other side of holiness. This story was documented by a television news magazine. A popular televangelist had his mail delivered to a bank where the money was taken out. The letters and prayer requests were not read but taken out back and put in the dumpster! Those prayer requests became a smell too—at the local dump! I believe in tithing and giving offerings but please check out who you give God's money to. I am not saying who to give offerings to, that's between you and the Lord. But when I was a new Christian I was supporting a TV preacher until I heard he had collected 80 million dollars in one year. I thought, "This guy doesn't need my offering, but I bet there is a smaller local ministry that does."

■ **Are people who present false Biblical beliefs using you? Why are these false teachers doing what they are doing?**

Those false teachers only want your money, so they will use you by telling you lies. II Peter 2:3

■ **Will there be world peace before the Prince of Peace (Jesus) comes back to earth? I wish the answer was yes, but Scripture says there will be wars until the world falls totally apart during the battle of Armageddon.**

You will hear about wars and stories of wars that are coming, but don't be afraid. These things must happen before the end comes. Matthew 24:6

You might have heard someone say, "I've read the last chapter of the Bible and we win." I just flipped the page to the beginning of Revelation and noticed what the sub-title read. "Christ will win over evil."

■ **What is the good news/bad news about the soon coming Tribulation period?**

After the vision of these things I looked, and there was a great number of people, so many that no one could count them . . . . They were all standing before the throne and before the lamb . . . . Then one of the elders asked me, "Who are these people dressed in white robes? Where did they come from?" I answered, " You know, sir." And the elder said to me, "These are the people who have come out of the great distress [Tribulation]. Revelation 7:9, 13, 14

Some people will turn to Jesus and be saved, but then most of them will be martyred for their new faith. Wouldn't it be a good idea to get right with God now prior to this terrible time?

■ **If all Christians are taken to heaven, who will spread the Good News of the gospel during the Tribulation period? Could it be Jewish people preaching the gospel of Jesus?**

"Do not harm the land or the sea or the trees until we [angels] mark with a sign the foreheads of the people who serve our God." Then I heard how many people were marked with the sign. There were one hundred forty-four thousand from every tribe of the people of Israel. Revelation 7:3, 4

There will be 12,000 Jews from each of the twelve tribes of Israel (144,000 total) preaching the gospel around the world during the Tribulation.

■ **The comet, Hale-Bopp, was fascinating to hear about and see with the naked eye. During the Tribulation period will something similar to it collide with the earth?**

Then the second angel blew his trumpet, and something that looked like a big mountain, burning with fire, was thrown into the sea. And a third of the sea became blood, a third of the living things in the sea died, and a third of the ships were destroyed. Revelation 8:8, 9

This verse reads like science fiction, but it is describing a huge comet or asteroid that plunges into the ocean sometime in the future.

■ **What three words found in the book of Revelation sum up what the Tribulation period has to offer?**

"Trouble! Trouble! Trouble for those who live on the earth . . . ."
Revelation 8:13

■ **It's hard to come up with encouraging items from the book of Revelation until the last few chapters. Most of the book has God dealing with sin and disobedience, and it's not pretty. Do things get so bad on earth that people would rather die than face another day?**

And the pain they felt was like the pain a scorpion gives when it stings someone. During those days people will look for a way to die, but they will not find it. They will want to die, but death will run away from them. Revelation 9:5, 6

■ **Am I naive or just Norwegian? Wouldn't you think most people on earth, during this terrible trouble, would put two and two together and decide to serve God instead of sin?**

The other people who are not killed by these terrible disasters still did not change their hearts and turn away from what they had made with their own hands. They did not stop worshiping demons and idols made of gold, silver, bronze, stone, and wood—things that cannot see or hear or walk. These people did not change their hearts and turn away from murder or evil magic, from their sexual sins or stealing. Revelation 9:20, 21

■ **The Jews are preparing to build their third temple, but the Islamic Dome of the Rock is on the thirty-five acre temple site. Most people believe Islam's third most holy site must be removed in order for the Jews to build their temple. Would it be possible to have them both on that site at the same time?**

But do not measure the yard outside the temple. Leave it alone, because it has been given to those who are not God's people. Revelation 11:1

There is enough room for both to coexist and I believe this Scripture leaves room for that possibility. So many things point to the fact that our generation will be the one to see Christ return. The third temple is not built until after the Rapture and the Jews are getting ready to build it right now! They already have most of the temple implements made and they are currently training priests who will work in the temple. This is just another piece of the puzzle that tells us we are very close to the Second Coming of Jesus!

■ **Is an inference made to satellite TV in the Bible? How will every nation "look" at two dead bodies lying in the streets of Jerusalem during the Tribulation?**

The bodies of the two witnesses will lie in the street of the great city where the Lord was killed . . . . Those from every race of people, tribe, language, and nation will look at the bodies of the two witnesses for three and one-half days, and they will refuse to bury them. Revelation 11:8, 9

■ **At the time of the Rapture Jesus comes down to call us home. Isn't it likely His words to us will be the same ones He uses to call the two resurrected witnesses to heaven?**

Then the two prophets [witnesses] heard a loud voice from heaven saying, "Come up here!" And they went up into heaven in a cloud as their enemies watched. Revelation 11:12

■ **Right now the devil does his dirty work on the earth but he doesn't live here. Guess who will be living on earth during the Tribulation period?**

The dragon [the devil] with his angels was thrown down to the earth. "But it will be terrible for the earth and the sea, because the devil has come down to you! He is filled with anger, because he knows he does not have much time." Revelation 12:9, 12

■ **It may be against a person's will to worship Christ, but like it or not if they don't worship Jesus Christ they WILL worship the Antichrist! God gives us a choice to worship him. Does the Antichrist offer the same choice?**

This beast [false prophet] stands before the first beast [Antichrist] and uses the same power the first beast has. By this power it makes everyone living on earth worship the first beast, who had the death wound that was healed. Revelation 13:12

■ **Why in the world would anyone worship the Antichrist?**

And the second beast does great miracles so that it even makes fire come down from heaven to earth while people are watching. It fools those who live on earth by the miracles it has been given the power to do. Revelation 13:13, 14

First, people are going to believe the Antichrist is the real Christ because he will be killed and then be resurrected just like Jesus! Second, his partner in deception, the second beast, the false prophet, will do supernatural miracles to fool people into believing it is God's power doing this.

■ **What happens to people who worship the Antichrist?**

"And the smoke from their burning pain will rise forever and ever. There will be no rest, day or night, for those who worship the beast and his idol or who get the mark of his name [666]." Revelation 14:11

These people are all killed within three and one-half years and then spend forever in hell.

■ **People will have an opportunity to accept the real Christ by the preaching of the two witnesses and the 144,000 Jews during the Tribulation. God doesn't want anyone to miss heaven, so as one last opportunity does He send an angel to spread the Good News?**

Then I saw another angel flying high in the air. He had the eternal Good News to preach to those who live on earth—to every nation, tribe, language, and people. He preached in a loud voice, "Fear God and give Him praise, because the time has come for God to judge all people. So worship God who made the heavens, and the earth, and the sea, and the springs of water." Revelation 14:6, 7

It's true, people who are not Christians and have not rejected the idea of salvation through Christ prior to the Tribulation will have the opportunity to be saved. However, people who knowingly said no to the truth of the gospel prior to the Tribulation will find it almost impossible not to believe the lies of the Antichrist and will be lost forever! Don't be caught in the situation where you will have waited too long to decide if you want Jesus as your Savior. As the Scriptures proclaim, "Today is the day of salvation." See prayer on page 132.

He [the Antichrist] will completely fool those who are on their way to hell because they have said "no" to the Truth; they have refused to believe it and love it, and let it save them, so God will allow them to believe lies with all their hearts, and all of them will be justly judged for believing falsehood, refusing the Truth, and enjoying their sins.   II Thessalonians 2:10-12 TLB

■ **What happens to the United States during this seven year period of trouble?**

"Ruined, ruined is the great city of Babylon!" Revelation 14:8

That verse, as an answer, probably didn't make any sense but read Allen Bonck's book, "America, the Daughter of Babylon," and you should be convinced, like me, that America is brought down in ruin. Information on his writing is in the Suggested Reading list at the end of this book. Some of these thoughts and answers probably sound rather incredible, but don't judge them as "this is nuts" until you have studied them yourself!

■ **Toward the end of all this terrible trouble [Tribulation period] the oceans, rivers, and springs of water turn to blood. What is the reason for this?**

"They have poured out the blood of your holy people and your prophets. So now you have given them blood to drink as they deserve." Revelation 16:6

■ **Would you give God and "A" or an "F" for the way he decided to pour out His anger on evil people?**

"Holy One, you are the One who is and who was. You are right to decide to punish these evil people . . . ." And I heard a voice coming from the altar saying: "Yes, Lord God Almighty, the way you punish evil people is right and fair." Revelation 16:5, 7

■ **Are wars caused by evil spirits?**

These evil spirits . . . go out to the kings of the whole world to gather . . . the kings together to the place that is called Armageddon in the Hebrew language. Revelation 16:14, 16

The human will is responsible for many past wars but according to this Scripture wars can be started by the influence of evil spirits.

■ **The troubles get progressively worse during the Tribulation, but just when it seems things can't get any worse, what happens next?**

. . . and a big earthquake—the worst earthquake that has ever happened since people have been on earth. The great city split into three parts, and the cities of the nations were destroyed . . . every island ran away, and mountains disappeared. Giant hailstones, each weighing about a hundred pounds, fell from the sky upon people. People cursed God for the disaster of the hail, because this disaster was so terrible. Revelation 16:18—21

We have relatives in Texas who know things happen in a big way in the Lone Star State, but ya'll surely can't top this hailstorm can you?

■ **What is the end of the story to this murder mystery for the false prophet and the Antichrist?**

The false prophet and the beast [Antichrist] were thrown alive into the lake of fire that burns with sulfur. Revelation 19:20

■ **Can you imagine finding yourself in hell with the demons laughing at you just because you allowed Satan to trick you?**

The angel did this so he [Satan] could not trick the people of the earth anymore until the thousand years were ended. After a thousand years he must be set free for a short time. Revelation 20:3

There are many who go to churches where everything looks Christian on the surface, but the true saving gospel of Jesus Christ is not preached. These people have been tricked by Satan. Excellent trick insurance is to read your New Testament.

■ As we near the end of the book of Revelation things are starting to look up. After the devil is released for a short time at the end of the Millennium, does he finally get his eternal reward?

And Satan, who tricked them, was thrown into the lake of burning sulfur with the beast and the false prophet. Revelation 20:10a

■ For people who are born once and die twice their first death takes them to the grave. Where does their second death take them?

The lake of fire is the second death. And anyone whose name was not found written in the book of life was thrown into the lake of fire. Revelation 20:14, 15

Many people have been tricked into believing they are going to party in hell with their friends—I have just one question. How do you keep ice in your glass in a lake of burning sulfur?

By the way, where is purgatory? I didn't find it in my Bible. I challenge you to find it in yours. Don't be tricked! Read your trick insurance policy.

If you are Catholic this statement by Hank Hanegraaff should challenge you to know why you believe what you believe. "The New Catholic Encyclopedia actually acknowledges that the doctrine of Purgatory is not implicitly stated in the Bible."

■ If an angel appeared to you, is it permissible to show respect by worshiping him?

But the angel said to me, "Do not worship me! I am a servant like you, your brothers the prophets, and all those who obey the words in this book. Worship God!" Revelation 22:9

■ Our eternal life will be enjoyed on the New Earth and in the new Jerusalem God creates for us. Will there be a new sun to shine on your new mansion and will it ever be night time on this new planet?

The city [the new Jerusalem] does not need the sun or the moon to shine on it, because the glory of God is its light, and the Lamb [Jesus Christ]

is the city's lamp. By its light the people of the world will walk . . .
there is no night there. Revelation 21:23-25

*When does time end? God created time in Genesis 1:1 (In the beginning
. . . . That's also when baseball began—in the big inning!) The
chronicle of future events are; the Rapture of the Church, the
Tribulation period and the Millennium. It's at the end of the Millennium
where time ends and eternity begins.*

■ **What book must your name be in for passage into the heavenly
new Jerusalem?**

Only those whose names are written in the Lamb's book of life will
enter the city. Revelation 21:27

*Your name is entered into the Lamb's book of life the moment you
accept Jesus Christ into your life as Savior. You must see this fabulous
city—procrastination stops here. The prayer you procrastinated over is
on page 132.*

■ **Would God go so far as to call someone a coward who doesn't
believe in Jesus?**

"But cowards, those who refuse to believe . . . ." Revelation 21:8

Chapter Ten

"Truth stands the test of time; lies are soon exposed."
Proverbs 12:19 TLB

■ **What does the One who knows the future say about your horoscope?**

You have advisors by the ton—your astrologers and stargazers, who try to tell you what the future holds. But they are as useless as dried grass burning in the fire. They cannot even deliver themselves! You'll get no help from them at all. Isaiah 47:13, 14 TLB

■ **How did Jesus triumph over the devil in his daily life on earth?**

Jesus answered him [the devil], "It also says in the Scriptures, 'Do not test the Lord your God.' " Matthew 4:7

Jesus used His knowledge of the Scriptures to deal with the evil one. You live in Satan's kingdom (he is god of this world). Do you have the proper knowledge to defeat the devil's attacks against you? The way to survive successfully in this world is to know what your Bible says. I am going to repeat this until you are a success. Have a disciplined Bible reading/study time and attend a church you have checked out where the members bring their Bibles with them.

■ **Once the Scriptures are deep in your soul, the things you used to think were important are really not. And things such as where people spend eternity become very important. My heart was heavy after watching coverage of the tragic death of Princess Diana. I was saddened by such a senseless death. After the initial shock, my** questions focused on her eternal state. I waited for the network broadcasters to answer my pounding questions. Was she a Christian? Did she testify of being born again? Did she ever say she took part of her day and studied the Bible? Did she ever talk about living in heaven someday? What church did she attend? Was she a faithful church attendee? Did she teach her sons the foundations of truth from God's word? Silence! My heart was bursting—I didn't hear one answer to all my questions. I heard ample things about her thirty-six years of life, but about her eternal state—nothing. You can read your newspaper and watch your television, but real life is found under a dusty book cover with the title, "The Holy Bible."

Don't brag about tomorrow; you don't know what may happen then. Proverbs 27:1

May I ask who is telling your kids about Jesus. And who is telling them how they should live according to the Bible?

Teach a child to choose the right path, and when he is older he will remain upon it. Proverbs 22:6 TLB

■ **Where is your homeland? The answer is easy if you have an eternal perspective.**

But our homeland is in heaven, and we are waiting for our Savior, the Lord Jesus Christ, to come from heaven. Philippians 3:20

Where you came from or are living now might be fantastic, but try imagining your future heavenly homeland.

■ **The world says, "Better not spank." The Scriptures say, "Better to spank." What do you say? Would the owners manual (the Bible) for created children have the correct answer in black and white?**

Foolishness is bound up in the heart of a child, But the rod of correction will drive it far from him. Proverbs 22:15 NKJV

Don't fail to punish children. If you spank them, they won't die. If you spank them, you will save them from death [hell]. Proverbs 23:13, 14

■ **How many people in human history have walked on water?**

. . . Jesus came to them, walking on the water. Jesus said, "Come." And Peter left the boat and walked on the water to Jesus. Matthew 14:25, 29

Since that time there have been no other occurrences of anyone walking on water.

■ **How important are the words in the Bible? Will you personally be judged by those words?**

"The word I [Jesus] have taught will be their judge on the last day." John 12:48

It seems ironic but only the people who have rejected the words of the Bible will be judged by them at the final judgment. Jesus took care of judgment for believers at the Cross.

"There is a judge for those who refuse to believe in me [Jesus] and do not accept my words." John 12:48a

■ **Is the first hint of the trinity found in the very first verse of the Old Testament?**

In the beginning God [Elohim] . . . Genesis 1:1

In the original language, Hebrew, the word for God is Elohim and it's a plural word! That means it's referring to more than one and we know from the New Testament that God is composed of God the father, God the Son and God the Holy Spirit.

Then God said, "Let us make human beings in our [emphasis added] image and likeness." Genesis 1:26

■ **Why did young David take five sling shot stones with him when he went out to fight Goliath?**

Then he picked up five smooth stones from a stream and put them in his shepherd's bag and, armed only with his shepherd's staff and sling, started across to Goliath. I Samuel 17:40 TLB

He may have just taken extra ammo or gutsy little David knew Goliath had four brothers.

■ **I heard this saying. Is it true? "From goo to the zoo to you."**

So God created human beings in his image. In the image of God he created them. He created them male and female. Genesis 1:27

From goo to zoo to you might sound funny, but that's what your school tax dollars are teaching your kids! Christian, have you considered running for the school board?

■ **Who was Jesus' closest friend?**

Since I [John, the apostle] was sitting next to Jesus at the table being the closest friend . . . . John 13:23 TLB

■ **Did it take science to discover the world was not flat or was it an ancient man inspired by God?**

God sits on his throne above the circle of the earth . . . . Isaiah 40:22

Isaiah penned these words nearly twenty-eight hundred years ago. It was just five hundred years ago that science was able to verify this!

■ **If your sins can be forgiven, why not take advantage of that and have the best of both worlds—be a Christian but live like the devil?**

Christ is pure, and all who have this hope in Christ keep themselves pure like Christ. I John 3:3

■ **Do you want to know if the church you go to is a good one to be attending? Throughout this book I have given signs of good and bad churches. This clue might prompt you to search for a good church. A probable sign of a lacking church is one that doesn't require its people to bring their Bible with them. People look for hot tips in the stock market. This was a hot tip in the church market. You're welcome.**

Know what his Word says and means. II Timothy 2:15 TLB

David T. Moore, host of "Moore on Life" radio program said, "If you are falling apart, your Bible probably is not. If your Bible is falling apart, you probably are not."

■ **If you separate a politicians personal life from his public duties, will the people under their rule suffer if they are not good moral people?**

When the righteous are in authority, the people rejoice, But when a wicked man rules, the people groan. Proverbs 29:2 NKJV

■ **What does a "form of godliness" mean in 1998?**

They will be conceited, will love pleasure instead of God, and will act as if they serve God but will not have his power. Stay away from those people. Some of them go into homes and get control of silly women who are full of sin and are led by many evil desires. II Timothy 3:4-6

When you see on television a politician and his wife in Washington, D.C. coming out of a church with Bible in hand, don't be fooled. Some have a form of godliness but the opposite to that is a true Christian. Please address your letters to my wife—she likes getting personal mail.

■ **Abortion is a hotly debated topic today. You might get hotly upset with this statement then: "If you are pro-choice you are anti-God." Is that statement true or false?**

To choose life is to love the LORD your God . . . . Deuteronomy 30:20

■ **Which is the only book out of sixty-six in the Bible that promises the reader a special blessing from the Lord just for reading and doing what it says?**

Blessed is he who reads and those who hear the words of this prophecy, and keep those things which are written in it; for the time is near. Revelation 1:3 NKJV

The books of the Bible are sometimes referred to as God's love letters to us. I know you would read a love letter from a special person in your life. God would love for you to read His love letters too.

■ Is the phenomenon of falling backward under the influence of the Holy Spirit a Biblical principal? These are the verses that support being "slain in the Spirit."

That blank space was intentional because there are no verses that support this practice. Remember the book title, "How to Win Friends and Influence People?" I don't imagine I am winning too many new friends because of some of the statements I've made. When a person stands up for Biblical truth there is a lot of room because the crowd is rather sparse. Read your trick insurance policy daily!

A book that should support the practice, "Dictionary of Pentecostal and Charismatic Movements" states, "There is no biblical evidence for the experience [slain in the Spirit] as normative in the Christian life."

■ Who is the angel of the LORD in the Old Testament?

The angel of the LORD did not appear to them again. Then Manoah understood that the man was really the angel of the LORD. Manoah said, "We have seen God . . . ." Judges 13:21, 22

No one has ever seen God the Father. The Holy Spirit is spirit, so God, the angel of the LORD, is none other than Jesus! The term, angel of the LORD, is not found in the New Testament because Jesus has been revealed to us as God in human form.

■ Did the dinosaur live millions of years ago before people as your school tax dollars teach? Or were they created a few thousand years ago <u>along</u> with humans? As you know by now the truth is in black and white in your Bible.

"Look now at the behemoth, which I made <u>along</u> [emphasis added] with you; He eats grass like an ox. He moves his tail like a cedar [tree] . . . . Job 40:15, 17 NKJV

Behemoth had to be a dinosaur because there is no living or fossil creature that has a tail like a cedar tree that eats grass! Contact Dr. Mace Baker, 2683 Rosebud Lane, Redding, CA, 96002, for more exciting proof along this line.

■ **Is the depiction of the devil in red leotards accurate?**

Then another wonder appeared in heaven: There was a giant red dragon [the devil] . . . . Revelation 12:3

Red, yes; leotards, no.

■ **What color are your sins?**

The LORD says, "Come, let us talk about these things. Though your sins are like scarlet, they can be as white as snow. Though your sins are deep red, they can be white like wool." Isaiah 1:18

■ **What color represents death and anarchy in Scripture?**

This time a red horse rode out. Its rider was given a long sword and the authority to banish peace and bring anarchy to the earth; war and killing broke out everywhere. Revelation 6:4 TLB

■ **Maybe you've asked God before and didn't get a speedy answer but if you are suffering, do you or do you not believe God can help you?**

They captured Manasseh, put hooks in him, placed bronze chains on his hands, and took him to Babylon. As Manasseh suffered, he begged the LORD his God for help and humbled himself before the God of his ancestors. When Manasseh prayed, the LORD heard him and had pity on him. So the LORD let him return to Jerusalem and to his kingdom. Then Manasseh knew that the LORD is the true God. II Chronicles 33:12, 13

■ **Why did these avoidable, terrible things happen to Manasseh?**

The LORD spoke to Manasseh and his people, but they did not listen [emphasis added]. II Chronicles 33:10

This book has been telling you how to get to heaven and to read your Bible. Have you been listening?

■ A large truck is bearing down on a disoriented soul in the middle of the road. You observe what is about to happen and fly into action to save the person from certain destruction. You become aware of many people going down a wide road that drops off into eternal destruction. Who will fly into action to save them?

"The gate is wide and the road is wide that leads to hell, and many people enter through that gate. Do to others what you want them to do to you." Matthew 7:13, 12

■ If you have read this far you must be thirsty to know God in a deeper, personal way. Consider making Max Lucado's prayer yours. "Father we want to see you and know you better. We ask you, Father to help us see Jesus and to deepen our faith upon seeing him more clearly."

I am the Alpha and the Omega, the Beginning and the End. I will give free water from the spring of the water of life to anyone who is thirsty. Revelation 21:6

■ If on the other hand you have read this far and are not sure that what the Bible says is right or wrong, consider what Mike Gendron of Proclaiming the Gospel Ministry has said. "In this life we can be wrong about a lot of things and still survive, but when this life is over, if we were wrong about God's only provision for our sin, we will perish into the eternal lake of fire for all eternity. It is far better for one to have never been born, than to die having never been born again of God."

Mr. Gendron has a ministry to Catholics. A complimentary copy of his newsletter can be obtained by writing to PO Box 940871, Plano, TX 75094.

■ Is every word of God true?

Every word of God is true. He guards those who come to him for safety. Proverbs 30:5

■ **Can you trust the words in the Holy Bible?**

"These words can be trusted and are true." Revelation 22:6

I heard a better definition of the word Bible, in an acrostic form, than even Webster could articulate.

> *B asic*
> *I nstruction*
> *B efore*
> *L eaving*
> *E arth*

■ **What is the last word in the Bible?**

The grace of the Lord Jesus be with all. Amen. Revelation 22:21

■ **Will I meet you in heaven? In the meantime:**

The grace of the Lord Jesus Christ, the love of God, and the fellowship of the Holy Spirit be with you all. II Corinthians 13:14

■ **I feel it only appropriate to close with a question. Did you notice the Trinity in the last verse?**

Notes

1. D. James Kennedy, *Truths That Transform*, radio program, March 31, 1998.
2. Mike Moskau, *How Do You Get to Zap, North Dakota?*, 7.
3. David T. Moore, radio program, *Moore on Life*, February 27, 1998.
4. David T. Moore, radio program, *Moore on Life*, February 27, 1998.
5. Mike Moskau, *How Do You Get to Zap, North Dakota?*, 7.
6. Video, "*The Earth, A Young Planet?*" Films for Christ, Mesa, AZ (602)894-1300.
7. *The New York Times*, February 1, 1990, B4.
8. Paul S. Taylor, *Origins Answer Book*, 42.

Suggested Reading

1. **America the Daughter of Babylon**
   The Prophetic Story of America's Future
   Author, Allen Bonck

Cost	$ 7.95
Shipping & Handling	1.00
TOTAL	$8.95

   Address:
   Allen Bonck
   6762 Xenon Drive
   Arvada, CO 80004

2. **How Do You Get To Zap, North Dakota?**
   A Road Map to Heaven
   Author, Mike Moskau

Cost	$ .75
Shipping & Handling	.75
TOTAL	$1.50

   Address:
   Mike & Linda Moskau
   PO Box 5172
   Golden, CO 80401

See next page to order *Solid Black and White Answers*.

Order Form

To order additional copies of *Solid Black and White Answers,* complete the information below.

Ship to: (please print)

Name _____

Address _____

City, State, ZIP _____

_____ copies @ $7.77 each...$ _____

Colorado residents add 4.3% tax of line above..................$ _____

Shipping & Handling: 1 book, $2.50 ....$ _____

    2-5 books, $6.00 ....$ _____

    6-10 books, $9.00 ....$ _____

Total amount enclosed ....$ _____

Make checks payable to Mike Moskau and send to:
Mike & Linda Moskau
PO Box 5172
Golden, CO 80401

- -

Order Form

To order additional copies of *Solid Black and White Answers,* complete the information below.

Ship to: (please print)

Name _____

Address _____

City, State, ZIP _____

_____ copies @ $7.77 each...$ _____

Colorado residents add 4.3% tax of line above..................$ _____

Shipping & Handling: 1 book, $2.50 ....$ _____

    2-5 books, $6.00 ....$ _____

    6-10 books, $9.00 ....$ _____

Total amount enclosed ....$ _____

Make checks payable to Mike Moskau and send to:
Mike & Linda Moskau
PO Box 5172
Golden, CO 80401